Jewish Clues
To Your
Health And Happiness

Jewish Clues
To Your
Health and Happiness

Sidney J. Jacobs, M.A.H.L., D.D.
Betty J. Jacobs, M.A.

JACOBS LADDER PUBLICATIONS
Culver City, California

First Edition

Copyright © 1990 by
Sidney J. Jacobs and Betty J. Jacobs

Library of Congress Catalog Card Number 89-64448
ISBN 0-933647-02-6

Printed in the United States of America
9 8 7 6 5 4 3 2 1

Contents

Appreciation

We thank Leslie Tryon, author and past president of the California Society of Illustrators, for her counsel on the design of this book. We thank Jean Stapleton, professor of journalism at East Los Angeles College, and William E. Evans, president of Evan-Moor Corporation of Monterey, California, for their advice on the production of this volume.

We are grateful to them, as we are to Joy Evans, Jo Ellen Moore, Marilyn Evans and J. Riley Fowler, Jr. for their continuing creative input, support and, most of all, their precious friendship.

About the Authors

Sidney J. Jacobs, M.A.H.L., D.D., is a rabbi and journalist. A valedictory graduate of Northwestern University's Medill School of Journalism, he began his professional writing career at the Chicago City News Bureau and went on to become an editor in Chicago and Los Angeles. He received his rabbinical ordination from the Hebrew Union College-Jewish Institute of Religion and has led congregations in Illinois, Minnesota and California. He is the author of *The Jewish Word Book* (1982) and co-author of *Clues About Jews For People Who Aren't* (1985) and *122 Clues For Jews Whose Children Intermarry* (1988).

Betty J. Jacobs, M.A., is professor of communications at West Los Angeles College in California. She is a media consultant and free-lance writer who has been the recipient of awards for television writing and production. She served as director of broadcasting for the Chicago Board of Rabbis and produced more than 600 television programs of Jewish content. In addition to the present volume, she is the co-author of *Clues About Jews For People Who Aren't* (1985) and *122 Clues For Jews Whose Children Intermarry* (1988).

Rabbi Sid and Betty live in Culver City, California, on the old MGM Lot #3 with their two dogs, Adam Randolph and Dodi-Li Daniel, and with Carlyle, a well-tempered computer.

Authors' Notes

The suggestions presented in this book will help many people lead happier and healthier lives. However, if you suffer from serious physical or emotional problems, we urge you to seek appropriate professional help.

In an effort to avoid sexist language, we have adapted some quotations instead of retaining their original wording. These adaptations are noted accordingly. We have not changed language where to do so would have destroyed the rhythm of the original.

English translations of verses from the original Hebrew of *The Holy Scriptures* are copyrighted and used by permission of The Jewish Publication Society.

SJJ
BJJ

Foreword

This book grew out of our conviction that you deserve to be as happy as you can, that you deserve good health and that you deserve to enjoy a feeling of self-worth.

Happy and positive-minded persons draw others to them. Happy people cope better with disappointment and even with tragedy. People want their company and their friendship.

We wrote this book, because we encounter so many individuals who feel either that happiness is an evasive, illusory goal or believe they could be happy if only their longing for riches could be satisfied.

The happiest people we have met are not famous, nor are they wealthy in terms of material possessions. They, too, have to face challenges of all sorts. What they do have is a splendid love affair with life.

This rapturous, ebullient approach to living can be yours. One person can make all this happen for you. That person is you.

This book is informed throughout by the spirit of Judaism. It could never have been written without the inspiration of Jewish sources: the Hebrew Bible, Mishnah, Talmud, Midrash, and the sages and commentators on these important, often sacred, works.

There are Jews who, because they lack a solid grounding in Judaism, see no purpose in remaining Jewish. They often look to Eastern religions or to the abundance of cults that flourish in our society with their promise that they can change our lives. They are addicted to pop psychologists on radio and television in an effort to pick up hints and morsels of help to being happier and enjoying life more.

Ironically, it is Judaism that has the answers to how to lead a happier life, reduce stress and improve relationships.

What does Judaism have to do with personal happiness? The stereotypes of the dour, fretting, guilt-shoveling Jewish mother, the carping and whining Jewish daughter and their sniveling, neurotic husbands and sons, which are the grist for so many "comedy" routines, only create a cloud over the real truth: Judaism is a faith whose teachings make for happiness and self-fulfillment.

This, then, is a book about health and happiness, derived from Jewish sources. You will find in its pages practical suggestions you can incorporate into your life now to sweeten your lifestyle and to make the time of your life truly Quality Time.

We would like to share with you the things we have found that make life good. We would like the days of your lives to be all that they can be. Adapt these clues to your own life and watch what happens. You have one life. Nurture it. Love it. Choose Life that you might live.

SJJ
BJJ

1

The Choice Is Yours

"I have put before you life and death, blessing and curse. Choose Life."

Deuteronomy 30:19

Lou is an affluent, retired businessman who takes an average of four cruises a year, where, he says, "I gamble, stuff myself and drink myself into a stupor to escape the four walls."

Trina is married to an accountant. Every day, Trina goes shopping. Her entire day focuses on the purchase of one item. Today it might be a blouse, tomorrow a set of place mats. Yesterday, she purchased a set of copper cookware, even though she hates to cook. Trina shops to keep busy. By the time she gets up in the morning, makes her decision about what to buy, decides where to look for the item, travels to the stores among which she will make her selection and executes the transaction, the major portion of her day is filled

Lynn, an attractive woman of 26, describes her existence as "blah and boring."

Gilbert, an insurance claims adjuster in his 40s, husband and father of three children, says happiness is impossible, and living means being unhappy.

15

We can't count the number of times we have heard people mutter that they will be happy when "this rotten day is over," "this dreadful week is past." And the weeks turn into months and years into decades, until life itself is over.

The news is filled with skyrocketing statistics of drug and alcohol abuse. Promiscuous sex is epidemic. We are taught to succeed in our professions by outmaneuvering our peers. We shun precious moments with our families to issue one more profit report. We scavenge the fancy car lots and designer clothing stores and crystal palaces for the possessions that we feel are due us for our labor.

We try to have power over things, because we feel we have none over ourselves.

So many good people tell us how they just seem to muddle through life without a passion for anything. The occasional highs they anticipate, the special vacation or celebration, are usually letdowns.

It doesn't have to be this way. You can be happy! You can have power over your life! You can control your destiny! You can know what it is to be truly content.

Judaism celebrates life. Instead of preaching predestination, Judaism presents you with choices. It was ever so, as far back as the Garden of Eden.

"And from the ground the Lord God caused to grow every tree that was pleasing to the sight and good for food, with the tree of life in the middle of the garden, and the tree of knowledge of good and bad."

Genesis 2:9

You are given one life. You may select all that is good in it or dwell on misfortune. You can create a reality that is a

16

celebration of life.

You may choose to enrich the blessing that is your life with improved health, friendship, knowledge, self-expression, the bounty of nature, the joy of helping others, the wise expenditure of the precious moments of your life.

"How sweet is the light, what a delight for the eyes to behold the sun! Even if a man lives many years, let him enjoy himself in all of them, remembering how many the days of darkness are going to be. The only future is nothingness."
Ecclesiastes 11:7-8

We can be sure of one thing: We have the moment! We can choose to imbue it with effervescence.

We are given one life, a magnificent opportunity to experience the world. Savor the gift.

"My cup runneth over."
Psalms 23:5

"Enjoy the honored vessel today: tomorrow it may be broken," we read in the *Talmud*.

Decide that you will honor your life. Decide that you will select your reactions to events, that you will establish your own values and etch out a bountiful existence.

"Whatever is in your power to do, do with all your might."
Ecclesiastes 9:10

You have the power to choose good, to choose life!

2

The Joy of
Positive Thinking

Your old men shall dream dreams, and your young men shall see visions."

Joel 3:1

Aunt Goldie and Uncle Seymour glared as if each had gulped an entire plate of bitter herbs at a *seder*. "This is the best they could do?" growled Aunt Goldie in the kind of hushed whisper everyone within an 11-foot radius at Barry's Bar Mitzvah could hear, even with the combo blaring out *Hava Nagila*.

Goldie and Seymour had wanted to be seated with Cousin Alex and Cousin Nancy and Cousin Max. Instead they were billeted next to Cousin Carole on Barry's mother's side and some other people they didn't know.

They huffed and puffed during the soup, salad, main course and dessert. They refused to dance. When Barry's parents, Hal and Jan, came over to the table to see how everything was going, they were treated to an earful. Auntie Goldie and Uncle Seymour told Barry that they hoped his becoming a Bar Mitzvah would make him a smarter person than his parents.

Aunt Essie also was surprised when she wasn't seated with the cousins. "It must have been a mess for Hal and Jan to figure out where to seat everyone. I'm going to help them have a wonderful party," she thought.

Essie introduced herself to everyone at the table. She was delighted with the new people she met. One woman had taken a trip to the Pennsylvania Dutch country that Essie was contemplating. She picked up a bunch of good hints. The woman told her the best time of year to go, a couple of great places to stay and a restaurant she should not miss.

Someone else at the table talked about a terrific lecture series at a nearby temple and offered to pick Essie up and drive her home, if she needed transportation. And with several college students at her table, Essie had the opportunity she'd been waiting for, to have someone explain the differences between rock and hard metal music. One of the students, a music major, explained everything and invited Essie to his graduation recital, scheduled for the following week.

When Hal and Jan came over to the table, Essie thanked them for providing her with the opportunity to meet all the interesting guests. She congratulated Barry and told him how lucky he was to have so many wonderful people celebrate with him.

Barry asked his parents if Aunt Essie could come over more often to visit.

Is something missing in your life? Do you feel you would be happy if you'd only land that position with the prestigious firm . . . or if you would fall in love . . . or if your daughter or son would be accepted by an Ivy League university. . . or if you had enough money to move to a larger house on that cul-de-sac in the seven-figure subdivision . . . or if you would win the lottery. . . or if you could take a trip around the world . . . or if your mate would bring you flowers and perfume. . . or if the kitchen sink didn't need to be repaired . . . or if the car didn't stall. . . or if you had the connections to record a hit music video?

Do you plan to be happy someday? Maybe . . . when you marry. . . when the raise comes through. . . when your children finish school. . . when the children get married. . . when you have grandchildren. . . when you retire?

There is always something undone. There is always something we want. There is always something . . .

"Someday" may never come. We have now, this moment. And we have a choice, to cherish it or damn it. We can choose to wallow in misery or bask in life. We can choose life!

Beginning right now, you can watch yourself metamorphose into a joyful, fulfilled, happy person who reaps the rapture of wonderful moments and who handles life's challenges with courage and strength.

You can choose to have a positive attitude. It's the attitude that you bring to every experience that determines the total experience for you. A positive attitude is portable. You can take it anywhere.

The person with a positive attitude doesn't look at horrible situations, roll his or her eyes and jubilantly announce that everything is wonderful. That person does look for the good in all situations and is able to sort out options in coping with the difficult ones. That person doesn't quibble about small problems but tries to solve them and views them as learning situations.

We all have dreams that have been shattered. We all suffer losses and hurts. These can make us bitter, cynical and hopeless, so that our attitude will compound the pain we experience. Or, we can choose to take our disappointments and channel our responses into positive energy.

The Joy of Positive Thinking

"This, too, is for good."

Talmud: Ta'anit 21b

Etta Byer was born in Lida, Poland, then under the rule of Czarist Russia. When she was 6, she was apprenticed to work in a cigarette factory. Her formal education ended within a year when the schools were closed to Jewish children, but she taught herself to read and write Hebrew and Yiddish from the books that filled her parents' home.

When she was 13, she escaped a pogrom in which a number of Jews were massacred. She managed to get to England, where she went to work in another cigarette factory. She labored 13 hours a day, making 3,000 cigarettes daily. Enrolling in a night school, Etta began her study of English.

She was adept at skirting the British child labor laws with her small, lithe body that could immediately duck under a table and crouch unnoticed until government inspectors left the room.

In the early 1900s, when she was 18, Etta sailed to the United States to join relatives. Cigarettes were now being made by machine, so Etta went to work in a cigar factory, instead. There she met her first husband The couple had three children, two sons and a daughter. Following the death of her first husband, Etta married Sam Byer, a prominent Jewish ethnic artist, and another son was born.

Etta went to work as a sewing machine operator in a leather manufacturing company. She called the factory her "university," because she learned so much about the different people who worked there. She considered the shop her second home.

When, at age 68, an economic recession cost her her job, Etta was despondent. Until, that is, she decided to take up what she called "pearl fishing."

"Pearl fishing" was Etta's search for knowledge and truth that took her to evening high school, where she enrolled in literature classes. She derived ecstasy from writers such as Walt Whitman, Willa Cather, Robert Frost and Sinclair Lewis. The night school was described by Etta as a holy temple, the perfect place for pearl fishing. Pearl fishing, she also explained, could be done at the public library, at museums, wherever people gather.

Etta, by then a widow who received an honorary high school diploma and was a busy writer and artist, was in her mid-80s when she attended our wedding in 1971 in Highland Park, Illinois.

Our move to California separated us from Etta until 1977, when we took a trip East. Etta was now living in a retirement hotel close to a son in New Jersey.

On the bus ride from New York City's Port of Embarkation to Plainfield, New Jersey, we speculated about what we might find. We weren't prepared for the "retirement hotel." The downstairs public room was drab and dark. A number of the residents stared into space. Others mumbled to themselves. Everywhere we looked, we saw crumpled bodies of sunken humanity slumped in chairs.

But, then there was Etta! She greeted us with a radiant smile, undimmed by the years or the circumstances.

After the tight hugs and kisses and tears, she guided us to her room. Etta had converted the tiny space into an airy, colorful artist's studio. Her pictures were everywhere. Colored pencils, paints, brushes and paper covered the surfaces of the dresser and night stand. Pictures of Etta's particular heroes, John F. Kennedy and Golda Meir, hung on the walls alongside Etta's art. She told us how lucky she was to have such a fine studio and how kind the staff of the hotel was to her.

In the midst of what appeared to be a gloomy setting, Etta was still pearl fishing. Etta Byer had chosen life!

"Hold on to resourcefulness and foresight. They will give life to your spirit."

Proverbs 3:21-22

Nora always wanted to marry and have children. When she was a teen-ager, she would carefully tape her dance bids, party favors, including printed napkins from Sweet 16 parties, matchbook covers and photographs, in large scrapbooks, "to share with my children" she would say, grinning as she pressed down another page.

Today, Nora is a bright, bouncy teacher. She admits that she became a teacher, because she felt this would be a career that would blend in with marriage and raising a family. But the years rolled along, and the right guy never showed. She dated frequently but didn't meet anyone with whom she wanted to build a life. And her biological clock ran out.

Is Nora miserable? No way! She's a delight to be with. In her mid-40s, she puts on a smile with every outfit. She purchased a small house several years ago and fixed it up like a country cottage. When you enter, you feel you've left the cares of the world behind. She lives there with Zeke, the smart, always wet-nosed German Shepherd-Lab mix she rescued from the local animal shelter, and Oscar, the slinky gray and white cat who popped up in her yard last year and decided to adopt her.

People have switched week-end travel plans to pull up chairs at her Sunday night "pasta-togethers," as she calls her mini-salons.

Her 12-year-old niece considers an occasional overnighter at

Aunt Nora's house a super treat.

When Nora eats alone, she plays classical cassettes, arranges flowers she plucks from her garden and lights beeswax candles, usually blue ones. After all, someone special is over for dinner. She is.

"From all of my students, I have learned something," says rabbinic Judaism. Betty learns constantly from her journalism students at West Los Angeles College. Don taught her a great deal. Don was in his mid-30s, working for a bill-collecting company, when he decided to go for a college education and become a journalist. He attended classes three nights a week, organized time he wasn't at work or in class into quality study time and covered major political meetings for the college newspaper. He had two indulgences: pizza and his red sports car.

He walked out of his apartment building one morning to discover that his car had been stolen. For a moment, his heart sank. Classmates to whom he reported the theft asked if he weren't frantic and depressed. Don said he was sure disappointed, but he did everything he could about his stolen car. He filed a police report, contacted his insurance company and rented a car. His day had been marred, but he didn't want to be marred himself He had enjoyed the car, realized he probably would never get it back, couldn't replace it, but he had to concentrate on other things like his career.

This positive attitude fortified Don as he wrapped up his studies at the community college, transferred to a university and landed a top job as a reporter for the *Fresno Bee*.

We had the privilege of meeting Dr. Bertha P. Dutton on our trip to Santa Fe, New Mexico, in the summer of 1989. She was then 86. An archaeologist, she came to the Southwest in 1932 and subsequently joined the staff of the Museum of New

Mexico. Three years later she became its Curator of Ethnology. After her retirement, she became director of the Museum of Navajo Ceremonial Art We asked this incredible woman, who dedicated her professional life to popularizing archaeology, if she had been denied positions because she was a woman. "Of course," she replied, "but I wasn't going to let them get me." Her feisty zest inspired everyone who was associated with her.

After their once-successful clothing store was plunged into bankruptcy, Murray and Sylvie knew they could no longer manage their upscale life in the fancy suburb. In their late 50s, they didn't see how they could rebuild the sumptuous lifestyle to which they had become accustomed. The spectacular house, imported sports cars, trendy clothes, parties, expensive continental restaurants, vacation cruises would quickly become memories. They studied their possibilities. With the little money they could salvage from the sale of the house and cars, they decided to move to a small town where they could afford a modest home. Sylvie, who had been a teacher before they opened the clothing store, got a job as a substitute teacher. Murray always enjoyed working with his hands but never had the time. He started whittling and chiseling small boxes and wooden toys and built bookcases and step-stools. These he took to art fairs in local parks and started to sell to stores. He has fine-tuned his craft to the point where people are hiring him to build bookcases in their homes.

Their house has a nice-sized yard where fruit trees are abundant. A vegetable garden provides squash, carrots, tomatoes and cabbage. The house is small enough, so Murray and Sylvie can hear when the other calls, something they could never do in their former home. They found a small synagogue that has just 65 families. They say they feel like newlyweds. By losing it all, they gained everything.

Neither a grouch nor a grumbler be. Stay positive. Do not let others pull you into their negative atmospheres. Do you ever get off the phone or return from a visit with someone where you feel lousy? Don't give in. Stay buoyant!

"A joyful heart makes a cheerful face. A sad heart makes a despondent mood."

Proverbs 15:13

People like people who have a positive attitude. It can be downright contagious. The person who has a smile for everyone, who sees life as an adventure, is like a pied piper. Everyone wants to get closer. These people light up a room. People are happy to see them, because they, in turn, are happy to see everyone. They make us feel good.

The late Rabbi David Graubart, who conducted our wedding ceremony, was like that. He always had a joke, a story, a pun to make you feel good. He walked into the room, and you knew it was going to be a good day, because he could put a smile on your face. He and his charming Eunice have enriched our lives.

Jewish history is rich with positive thinking, although some self-deprecating Jewish screenwriters and novelists have stomped out the image of Judaism as a positive faith and replaced it with a Judaism of neurotic guilt-trippers.

It was a positive attitude, a refusal to give up, a dedication to choosing life which made Jews who escaped persecution and annihilation rise out of the muck and mire and nourish life into the barren desert of modern Israel. Jews have not forgotten the striking imagery of the Prophet Ezekiel's vision of the Valley of Dry Bones. "Can these bones live?" Yes, indeed, they could -- and they have!

It was a positive attitude that gave Jewish immigrants fortitude, as they traveled in steerage to America, lived in crowded slums and worked for paltry wages in sweatshops. They knew,

27

so long as they had their health and the family was together, life was good. And it would be even better for their children, who would get the education Jews so valued.

"A joyful heart makes for good health. Despondency dries up the bones."

Proverbs 17:22

Making the best out of a bleak situation is an art so many Jews have perfected. It was winter, Hanukkah, in the Buchenwald concentration camp. The children wanted a *hanukkiah*, a Hanukkah menorah, and there was none to be found. Rabbi Frank Rosenthal, who would later serve until his death as the rabbi of Temple Anshe Shalom in Olympia Fields, Illinois, held up his fingers, placed matchsticks under the nails and lit them. When there was no menorah, this fine rabbi's hands became one.

Jews are encouraged to choose life. A Jewish wedding goes on, even if there has been a death in the family.

Judaism says that one week after a death, the mourners are to walk around the block to symbolically rejoin the world, to choose life.

They had been married for 54 years. The widow was 83 years old. She wept quietly as Sid recited the prayers and delivered the eulogy at her husband's funeral. As the casket was being lowered, Sid caught the glimmer of a smile on the elderly widow's wizened face, the tears still streaming down her high cheek bones.

"Was that a special smile for Ben?" Sid asked as they walked away from the interment site. She nodded. "Rabbi," she said, "God sent me a treasure and let me bask in it for 54 years. Now God has reclaimed my treasure. Do you know how fortunate I am, Rabbi, to have had my Ben? I look at all the young people.

28

So many will not find love. So many will mistake status for love, and they will find sorrow. I have been blessed.

"I grieve. My heart is twisted. My life will never be the same. I must go it alone. I'll never get over missing my Ben'eleh. But I, Rabbi, I am one of the lucky ones." Sid knew Ben had been one of the lucky ones, too.

It is not always the dramatic or tragic events that prove a challenge to our positive response. Often, it is the "whimpers" rather than the "bangs," the petty gridlocks of daily living, that try our patience and require our up-beat reaction.

You have choices to make. You can whine your way through life, playing the role of the victim You can grumble, grimace, sulk, scowl and jitter, fine-tuning your morose attitude into a prized speciality that you can haul everywhere. You can tabulate all of your misfortunes, keep score of all your grudges by tallying all those who have done you wrong, thereby multiplying the negative impact.

Or, you can raise your head high, delight in your joys, and turn your trials into triumphant learning experiences.

Rouse yourself! Wake Up and Live. Bask in the adventure of your life, and watch the changes that occur. The choice is always yours. Choose life!

3

You're Terrific!

You are unique. You are valuable. You are a treasure. Never before in history has there been someone exactly like you. Never in the future will there be another person exactly like you.

Rabbi Hillel, outstanding sage and personality, lived and taught at the beginning of the Common (Christian) Era. The tractate, "Ethics of the Fathers," in the Mishnah, the earlier part of the Talmud, cites him as teaching:
>"If I am not for myself, who is for me?
>"If I care only for myself, what am I?
>"If not now, when?"
>
> *Pirke Avot 1:14*

In *Leviticus 19:18*, the instruction is that "You shall love your neighbor as yourself." The Ba'al Shem Tov ("Master of the Good Name"), founder of the Hassidic movement in Judaism who lived during the first half of the 18th century, enlarged on this verse in the Hebrew Bible by saying that before you can love your neighbor you must be able to love and accept yourself.

He pre-dated by two centuries the Jewish psychoanalyst, Erich Fromm (1900-1980), who advocated learning to love ourselves before we can successfully love others.

You're Terrific!

Yet, so many people spend so much of their lives in self-deprecation. We have met people from all walks of life, some considerably successful in terms of public recognition and material wealth, who have told us of the emptiness they feel inside, the feeling that they are phonies and their fear that someone will find out. Many disguise their lack of confidence in bravado and in appearing to be snobbish to others, because they fear exposing their true selves.

Some accumulate caches of clothes, jewelry and other worldly possessions to fend off the feelings of inferiority, hoping the world will buy the image of success and not notice the quivering humanity hiding under the designer labels.

So long as a person imagines that he or she cannot do a certain thing, it is impossible for them to do it, observed the Jewish philosopher, (Baruch) Benedict Spinoza (1632-77).

Procrastination becomes an easy out for men and women, boys and girls, who lack the confidence that they can do a job.

You deserve happiness! You deserve to feel good about yourself. You deserve to treat yourself as you would treat others, and as you would like to have others treat you: with respect, warmth and love.

"How can one be merciful to others who is merciless to oneself?" asked the early 13th century Hebrew poet of Barcelona, Abraham ben Samuel ha-Levi ibn Hasdai. Makes sense, no? If you do not cherish yourself, how can you cherish others?

Having self-esteem means understanding that you can make a difference in the world. Every good deed you perform makes the world better. The potential for good is within you. The promise of the Messianic Age is in you, in every one of us who understands that we are able to release the good within us.

You have the power to start movements that will eradicate suffering, just as you have the power to say "Good Morning" to a lonely neighbor. Don't neglect one, because you aren't going to do the other. A better world begins with simple things. Everything you do makes a difference.

An afternoon talk show on national television featured a Jewish woman and her daughter-in-law, who were willing to air the difficulties in their relationship before millions of viewers. One of the major issues that arose was the mother-in-law's discontent over where she was placed at holiday gatherings. Honor was shown, she said, according to how close to the front of the table one was placed. She was placed close to the end.

If we enter a situation loving ourselves and ready to love those around us, are we going to dwell on table placement? Are we going to persist in setting up situations in which we are doomed to lose?

Does that mean that we should never express our feelings? Of course not. If you have confidence in yourself, you can eject yourself from unsalvageable situations, stuffy dinners, whatever. You can say "no" graciously.

So many people live lives of internalized despair and unvoiced anxiety, tormenting themselves because they are waiting for others to approve of them, for others to make them happy.

Many of us were never nurtured as children and don't know how to nurture ourselves. As grownups, we have to understand that each one of us is worthy of nurturing.

A lack of self-esteem not only creates unhappiness, because it makes us feel inferior to others and victimized by life, but it can be downright dangerous.

Alcohol and other addictive substances are used to soothe the ache caused by a lack of self-worth. Many who lack confidence seek out destructive personal relationships, clinging to men and women who treat them shabbily, because they themselves lack self-worth.

Corinne reports one affair after another in which she was treated like "dirt." Several men have borrowed money they never paid back. One walked off with her brand new 35mm camera. Another moved into her condo for two years, never paid a penny in rent and expected her to have dinner on the table every night and to do his laundry. Another ran up whopping long-distance phone bills whenever he dropped in for a visit. Why doesn't she hold out for a guy who will treat her with kindness and respect? She's afraid, she says, to be without a man. What will people think?

Nowhere is self-esteem so tested than at "singles" dances, where good and lovely -- and lonely -- men and women put themselves on the block to be gazed over for superficial qualities that might satisfy someone's preconceived notions of the ideal male or female. To build confidence, a person is far better off pursuing his or own special interests in hiking parties, discussion groups and causes where people really get to know each other.

Again, remember what Hillel said, "But if I am for myself alone, what am I?" The person who doesn't understand his or her own need for love and caring can't comprehend these needs in others and has difficulty showing emotions.

Rex has been dying inside for 35 years, ever since he was a little boy. A muscular six-footer with rugged features and a shock of jet black hair, he's been a "ladies' man" since the girls started asking him out in fifth grade. A brash whiz kid, he easily glided through elementary and high school, struggled slightly in college and was almost diligent in law school. He was so flattered for his looks and brains that he feared that if people saw the real Rex they wouldn't like him. So, Rex has become a snob. He puts up a wall with people and only turns on the charm if someone can do something to benefit him, sexually or in business.

If you meet Rex at a party, you will probably find him to be conceited, totally disinterested in you. If you can get him to talk, he will be glib about his success as an attorney, and he'll tell you about his coming trip to Tahiti, his fourth in three years. If you're bent on sharing your experiences, forget it. What Rex won't tell you is that he lies on a therapist's couch three times a week, snorts cocaine and has no close friends.

There is a familiar anecdote in Yiddish folk literature about a simple Jewish workman of limited education and even more meager income who becomes depressed as he grows older and feels that he has not achieved anything in life. He seeks the counsel of a village elder, who speaks to him in this way:

"Reb Shmerel -- you should live to be 120 years! -- when you pass on and appear before the Throne of Justice, God will not ask you, 'Shmerel, my son, why weren't you like Moses the Lawgiver in your lifetime, or like the Ba'al Shem Tov, or like the Dubner Maggid?' The Almighty will ask only one question: 'Dear Reb Shmerel, why were you not like -- Reb Shmerel? Why did you not live up to your full potential during your lifetime?'"

"No tongue speaks as much ill of us as our own," observed Sholom Aleichem (1859-1916), the "Jewish Mark Twain."

Do not punish yourself by hurting others. Don't shove them away by sending signals that you don't want them around.

Don't let others define you. Define yourself in terms of your own interests and goals. We see so many young people at pivotal points in their development searching for role models and who attempt to make themselves clones of film and television personalities, rock stars, sports heroes and, sometimes, fellow students who appear to have it all together. "If only I looked like her, everyone would like me," a teen-ager speculates, not realizing that her idol of the moment is a packaged commodity designed to sell movie seats and compact discs.

The advertising industry thrives on lack of consumer self-esteem. We are offered shampoos, soaps, diet soft drinks, perfumes, hair dyes, deodorants, mouthwashes and tooth-pastes that will enchant others and make us acceptable and perhaps loved by them.

Listen to the commercials. Analyze the messages. They're selling us love, self-esteem and success. The media mavens who plot these glitzy sales pitches know full well that many people lack self-esteem, because they don't consider themselves thin enough or attractive enough.

In a Thai restaurant, we were unscheduled spectators of lunch between two men in their 40s. One was obviously ill at ease and desperately trying to impress the other. His body language gave him away. He slouched over his food, folded and unfolded his hands under the napkin that lay on his lap and then proceeded to fumble with the chopsticks. At the end of the meal, he stood up, looked into the eyes of his luncheon partner and delivered his image-rescuing salvo, "You have to see my new car. I spent $60,000 on that beauty. It's got everything!"

Sophie lived in a sprawling five-bedroom house in a fancy suburb. Her two children were enrolled in expensive private schools. She was always up on the latest hair designer, hired the hottest caterers, enlisted an interior decorator who had landed a spread in a major architectural monthly, wore the latest fashion and almost toppled over when Arnold, the super-provider, the husband with whom she hadn't had an intimate conversation in years, left her for someone Sophie calls "a graying, brown-haired twit, who wouldn't know a French design if it wrapped itself around her neck."

Sophie had bought the media advertising pitch. She hadn't paid attention to the venerable Yiddish saying, "*ess veht ihr helfen vee ah toiten bahnkess,* " "it will help her as much as 'cupping' (blood-letting) will benefit a corpse."

"To please all is an impossible aim, and to escape criticism is an unattainable goal," wrote Moses ibn Ezra (1055-1135), Spanish Jewish philosopher and poet.

We are each endowed with different traits, pursue different interests, develop different talents. How can we compare ourselves with others?

We strive to be accepted by everyone else. We recoil at the least show of rejection. The most important person to be accepted by is yourself. You should have the ability to laugh at yourself when you fumble instead of feeling humiliated. Only you can determine your response.

When you have self-esteem, you don't have to validate someone else's rejection of you -- whether in a job loss or in a romance. These might be disappointing, but they need not be ego-shattering.

Having self-confidence allows you to follow your own path, even when you are in the minority. You have ability to make decisions, to have values when others aren't certain about theirs.

Jennifer Graham was a high school student when she drew national media attention because she bucked the teasing of

classmates and reprisals by school officials, because she refused to dissect a frog in a biology class. A top student and a
vegetarian who believes in the sanctity of all life, Jennifer
offered to substitute another project to prove her knowledge of
a frog's anatomy. Jennifer is a poised and articulate young
woman who knows who she is.

"If not now, when?" Why not start loving yourself . . . today. . .
right now . . . this minute?

Throughout your life, you are the person with whom you will
share the most intimacy. You can decide whether to imbue this
person over whom you have charge with love and compassion
or to withhold these riches. You can make that person happy
or miserable. You can treat that person honestly, critically
when you err, or tear that person down. Begin to love yourself
right now. Rejoice in your gift of life. Understand that every
experience you have makes for growth.

When you have self-confidence, you can reach your potential.
You are able to take an objective, personal inventory, noting
your strengths and your weaknesses.

You do count for something! You deserve good things: beauty,
art, music, friendship, love, happiness. Today you are experi-
encing the greatest gift of all: life. Enjoy it! Celebrate! Turn
on some music. Set flowers on the dinner table; yes, even if you
are dining alone. Prepare your favorite delicacy, and put on
your happiest face. Take control of your destiny. Remember,
you deserve it!

4

Setting Goals

"Let your eyes look forward,
Your gaze be straight ahead.
Survey the course you take,
And all your ways will prosper."

Proverbs 4:25,26

You don't have to let life's events fall on top of you. You don't have to go around with your head lowered, ready to duck the next swat from the world.

You can take responsibility for your life; you can direct it. The more you are in control of your life, the happier you are.

Establishing goals is a definite way of taking control. Establishing goals means considering realistic options, taking action, creating change to enhance your life and solving problems.

Establishing goals is choosing life. We can meet our goals by identifying them, then listing the steps we must take to meet each goal.

Reva decided to read all the books written by Joyce Carol Oates. She did, one at a time, over a six-month period. You can familiarize yourself with the works of Isaac Bashevis Singer or Virginia Woolf. You could tackle the entire writings of William Shakespeare.

Your goal might be to have your own vegetable garden. Marshall and Esther decided to have one. They measured the size of the plot they would have. They talked to people in their neighborhood about the types of vegetables that would grow best in their climate. They decided to start with four of their favorites for salad: tomatoes, cabbage, carrots and zucchini. They drew up a shopping list and shopped for seeds and for tools. Then they tilled, hoed, seeded, weeded, snipped, watered and plucked.

Joe is a pianist who's immersed in writing a book about music. The day we spoke to him, he had been up for 24 hours, too excited and bursting with ideas to leave his project for bed. Joe's goal is to complete this book, and to follow it with three more. When he will have finished, he wants to learn all he can about computers. Joe is 81.

The most successful retirees are those who establish new goals. Because our careers fulfill social as well as economic needs, experts deem it desirable to refocus at retirement.

Some retireees become students again. Many commit to causes and issues. A Michigan teacher who retired in 1986 turned his interest in organic gardening into a full-time commitment to environmental issues. He belongs to 35 organizations, sits on the executive board of one, demonstrates, writes letters and mobilizes community support.

The important thing is to plan, to set goals, not to create situations in which you feel unwanted and unneeded.

"Be pliable like a reed, not rigid like a cedar."
Talmud: Taanit 20b

Part of establishing goals that you can meet means assessing where you are now. Your goal might be to finish a 10k run. If you don't run at all, you will have to start with very short distances. Running down the block might be your first step. If you're just starting to get in condition, you might have to begin by walking, building up to fast walking, then jogging or sprinting short distances. If you run three miles regularly three times a week, you can train for the 10k by pushing for longer distances on one of those runs.

A favorite goal-setting story of ours is about Faye, who committed herself to a goal that would radically change her life. She decided to become a lawyer.

People smiled when she announced her goal. Her sister thought it was bizarre. At 48, Faye had raised a family and hadn't attended school in 29 years.

Faye was undaunted. She first had to earn her bachelor's degree. She phoned a counselor at a nearby state college and set up an appointment. The counselor listed the courses in the pre-law curriculum. Faye applied to the college but wasn't accepted, because her test scores weren't high enough. But her goals were.

So, she enrolled at a community college, where she took a workshop geared to helping returning students brush up on study skills. Realizing that she was part of a growing population of women and men returning to college after many years, Faye's confidence was restored.

After sweating English and math placement exams, Faye didn't groan for a moment when she found out she would have to take an English preparatory class to ready her for the basic course required for her degree. She pursued that course one essay at a time, building her grammatical, vocabulary and spelling skills as she went. Her organization tightened up.

Her writing began to flow. Her confidence soared.

After completing all of her general education requirements, she applied to and was accepted by a four-year college. Now, she was ready for it.   Two and-a-half years later, she was marching in the commencement processional.

She entered law school a couple of months later. Knowing how tough this last phase of her education would be, she formed a study group. Her perseverance drove her through law school, the bar exam, her first job and, today, a junior partnership in a growing law firm.

Faye attained her goal by identifying the necessary steps and taking them one at a time.

Your goals need not be so grandiose. Setting goals you can successfully meet almost immediately can clear your mind to surmount traumatic problems.

The day when Gladys realized that a reshuffling which might cost her her job was underway at the company she'd been working for she went home in an emotional frazzle. Determined to take out her frustration on something tangible, she attacked her bedroom closet. She pulled out everything and set it all on the bed and the floor: the clothes, the suitcases, the shoes, the boxes of forgotten stuff. She sorted out the blouses, dresses, skirts, jackets and pants that she hadn't worn in years. All those "you never know" things that she hadn't worn for three years were piled into a stack for rummage sales. Her good things she divided by item and color. She hung her two long-sleeve, blue blouses next to each other, with the one short-sleeve, blue blouse next to them.   It was a rigorous overhaul of her clothing landscape.

By the time she finished, her closet had been converted into an organizer's paradise. Gladys felt in control.   Exhausted from the closet caper, she had a good night's sleep. The next morning, refreshed and clear-thinking, she was able to consider her options in the face of a possible job loss. She pulled out her resume and scribbled notes on it, just in case. She drafted a list of companies where she might apply for work. She even made some notes about other cities where she might like to live. All of this she placed in her just-in-case file.

Setting goals can save your family relationships. Setting goals, controlling your life can save your life.

Sally figured this out before it was too late. Her goal was to distance herself from her abusive husband. The first step was to admit she had a problem. Her second step was to ask for help, something she was embarrassed about at first. Desperate after David punched her out, leaving a black eye and her legs black and blue from where he had swung a baseball bat, she contacted the Jewish Family Service office in her city.

She was referred to a special project for abused wives, where she found out that Jewish men are as capable of socking women as anyone else. And that wives of businessmen, lawyers, doctors, judges and rabbis are not immune from this menace.

Sally's husband was offered counseling. He refused it, maintaining that Sally was the problem, that her nagging so unnerved him that he had to belt her on occasion. He actually almost had her convinced that the beatings were her fault until he almost killed her. Strengthened by the counseling, she filed criminal charges against him and filed for divorce.

Sally learned that saying "I need help" is a life-affirming goal.

We were shocked when a colleague of Betty's, a brilliant community college professor, described her husband's beatings of her and her son. After the second beating binge, during which he broke several of her ribs, she threatened to embarrass him publicly by divulging his actions. He stopped. This highly-educated man enjoys a national reputation in his field. His outward appearance is that of an energetic, witty, gentle, generous man. Only his wife and her son experienced his rage.

"I probably deserved it, " she said, "I can be a real pain."

Now, hear this! Under no circumstances do you deserve to be injured by another person. You are precious. You were not born to be a punching bag.

Ignoring abuse is a dangerous game of self-deception. Get yourself out of dangerous situations. Get your children out of dangerous situations. The person who is hurting you needs help. If he or she refuses to get it, leave. If the situation is out of control, leave. If drugs or alcohol turn that person into a tragedy waiting to happen, leave.

Do not concern yourself with what your friends or family will think. Find out your legal rights. Join a support group for people who have had the same experiences.

Do not allow yourself to be battered. Choose life!

Your goal can be to start a new hobby. Your goal can be to switch careers. You can join a cause. You can improve your health. You can begin a painting or a quilt or a sculpture. You can learn about a new subject. Every chapter in this book offers ideas for goals you might want to set. Your goal can be to save your life.

What are your dreams, your goals? Only one person can achieve your goals for you. You!

Having goals makes us feel invigorated with life. Maybe that's why so many Jews set goals on Rosh Hashanah, the Jewish New Year. The "birthday of the world" is a perfect time to make resolutions. This two-day holiday (one day for Jews of the Reform persuasion) in September or very early October of each year is a time not of the hoopla associated with the secular New Year of January 1 but a period for introspection and the setting and re-setting of personal goals.

Choose to have goals. There are classes to take, degrees to earn, paintings to paint, poetry to write, fields to hike, causes to help, gardens to plant, beaches to comb. skills to master, books to read, parks to stroll, people to meet. . .you to love.

5

To Your Health!

You deserve excellent health.

You deserve that incredible feeling of well-being that comes from having a body in harmony with itself.

You deserve the energy that allows you to plunge into life's adventures with gusto.

You deserve the feelings of exaltation and exhilaration that allow you to work and play your best.

You deserve the sound sleep, sexual potency, muscle tone, clear, glowing skin, sparkling eyes, rosy cheeks and shiny hair, the attractive body that beams with good health.

You also deserve the freedom from high medical costs, dependency upon side effect-producing pharmaceuticals and worry that you might become the next victim of a debilitating and life-threatening disease.

Maimonides, the great Jewish physician and philosopher of the 12th century (1135-1204), wrote in his *Guide for the Perplexed*, "The well-being of the soul can be obtained only after that of the body has been secured."

To Your Health!

How meaningful those words become when our health or the health of a member of our family is in jeopardy. How many times have we heard people say, "I would gladly renounce every thing I own, if only my husband would recover." Think of the stress you have suffered during periods of severe family illness.

Good health isn't a matter of luck. You do have control over your body. By making the proper choices, you can trade in a sluggish body that causes pain and makes you irritable for a vigorous one that allows you to enjoy every moment more.

The fundamental ingredient to achieving radiant health is the food we eat.

Selecting that food is no longer a mystery. Your basic shopping list has been prepared for you and presented to you in the Hebrew Bible! There, in the Book of *Genesis,* God said. "See, I give you every seed-bearing plant that is upon the earth, and every tree that has seed-bearing fruit: they shall be yours for food.....of every tree of the garden, you may freely eat...and you shall eat the grains of the field." *(1:29, 2:16, 3:18)*

That this plant-based diet should be featured in *Genesis* is really amazing. It is the diet that progressive epidemiologists, nutritionists and physicians are recommending for health and longevity as we approach the 21st century. The grain-centered, fiber-rich diet, which epidemiological and clinical studies have indicated reduces the risks of heart disease, hypertension, most cancer, multiple sclerosis, tumors, kidney disease, osteo-porosis, diabetes, arthritis and other degenerative disease, is thousands of years old.

This is the high-fiber, low-fat diet that contains all of the protein, calcium and other minerals and vitamins needed not only to sustain life but also to prevent the ghastly diseases unique to a society that gorges on animal foods, white flour products and refined sugar.

Many vegetarian nutritionists recommend taking a Vitamin B-12 supplement.

This is the health-maintaining, vegetarian diet that not only can keep us safe from treacherous degenerative diseases but can also protect us from minor but annoying health problems that gnaw away at our moods and productivity, problems such as overweight, impotence, dental caries, stomach aches, headaches, colds, sore throats and irritability.

It is also the violence-free diet that reduces animal suffering and can help ameliorate world hunger. The ecologically sound diet that makes for a healthier us also makes for a healthier earth!

Cuisine free of animal products is not only nutritious but delicious and money-saving.

Everyone at the table had three servings of everything the night we brought out heaping dishes of buckwheat and whole wheat pasta tossed with extra virgin olive oil, chopped vine-ripened tomatoes, fresh basil, crushed garlic and sliced mushrooms; carrot and cabbage slaw and tofu banana pie -- mashed tofu mixed with mashed bananas, doused with cherry cider and spiked with pure vanilla.

A Sunday night dinner at our home, shared with good friends, led off with crisp crudites -- carrots, celery, zucchini, mushrooms, cherry tomatoes, green onions and broccoli -- heaped on a 20-inch, stoneware plate. A tangy, tofu dill sauce was there for the dipping. Steaming bowls of zesty lentil chile followed, together with sides of golden brown rice. Slices of apple baked with vanilla and cinnamon and a few squirts of pure apple juice on a bed of rolled oats was served for dessert. The meal was tasteful, peaceful and warming.

Many people who have switched to this complex carbohydrate diet wonder why they didn't get into it long ago. Once you delight in the scrumptious fare, you'll love it.

Try barley soup, brown rice and a wok of vegetables, grain burgers, whole grain pasta, millet and vegetable casseroles, bean soups and stews, stuffed baked potatoes, pita bread pocket sandwiches, grain and vegetable loaves. Try snacking on popcorn, nuts and seeds (some people soak them for easier digestion), baskets of oven "fried" potatoes (sliced thin and baked to a crispy texture), rice cakes with peanut butter, cut-up vegies and whole grain toast sliced into squares. Tantalize your taste buds with ethnic treats such as tostadas, spaghetti, curry. Health food stores feature tofu hot dogs and a variety of burgers. Just remember to keep the vegetable fats such as nuts and oils to a minimum.

Scour your bookstore for vegetarian recipe books to help you make the transition.

The eating-out problem is solved with the proliferation of salad bars as well as restaurants whose menus list baked potatoes, steamed vegetable plates and pasta with marinara sauce. For variety, seek out Chinese, Indian and Thai restaurants that serve up noodles or rice with vegetables flavored with unique spices. Israeli restaurants make terrific hummus, mashed garbanzo beans with spices, lentil dishes and eggplant speci-alities.

Many cities boast of at least one vegetarian restaurant. We're lucky that Los Angeles even features one that is gourmet, vegetarian Chinese -- with the erstwhile chef of a Buddhist temple, no less, presiding over its kitchen.

On a driving trip last summer through Arizona and New

Mexico, in the land of cowboys, we fared very well. One of the most sumptuous of salad bars was available at a massive truck stop in Ash Fork, Arizona. We parked our "rig" (a 1985 Volvo with the unlikely name of "Shainkeit," Yiddish for "cutie-pie") and hightailed it into a trucker's paradise complete with TV viewing areas, showers, gift shop -- and the 20-foot salad bar.

At establishments in the Southwest, where the offerings were less grand, we dined happily on baked potatoes with barbecue sauce and dinner salads. In Santa Fe, New Mexico, the splendid art colony and oldest U.S. state capital 7,000 feet up at the foot of the Sangre de Cristo mountain range, we found a splendid, gourmet, macrobiotic cafe.

Our eating style is fun, inexpensive, energizing, healthy, and it keeps both of us slender.

So many people we know have become disenchanted with strict regimens in which you measure four ounces of this, slathered with a level, half- teaspoon of that, capped with two square inches of something else. We have watched good people torture themselves for days, weeks and, in some cases, for months, usually in a majestic effort to shed pounds.

With rare exceptions, even the most impressive weight losses are temporary, because no change of lifestyle occurs. On the other hand, a foodstyle devoid of animal products allows the body to lose weight naturally and keep that weight off. We wish you could meet every person we know who has made this change.

One day, while pouring millet into bags in a health food store on Beverly Boulevard in Los Angeles, we were interrupted by a sweet voice asking if we could reach up for a package of stone-ground, whole wheat bagels. As we handed the bagels over, we were struck by the woman's complexion. She had skin as smooth as alabaster, etched with just a few wrinkles. Her blue eyes were clear. She wore no lipstick, and yet her lips were rich with color. Her white hair was thick and lustrous. Her posture was perfect, her voice vibrant. She had asked us to reach for the bagels only because we were blocking her path.

She was 93! For the past 50 years, she said, she had been eating a diet in which brown rice, whole wheat, barley, oatmeal and beans were her staples. She ate no animal products. She proudly told us that in all that time she had never been ill. She was happy and excited about life.

How many times have you heard that you are what you eat? Your food really does become part of you. A friend of ours reported that one day she gazed over her dinner plate of meat, greasy potatoes, white rolls and sugar-glazed carrots served up on fine china in a trendy restaurant. (This glop had a high price.) She imagined the contents of her plate flowing through her system and decided right then and there to switch to what she calls her "grain and green" style of eating. Friends who haven't seen her in a while say she looks years younger. A colleague at work teases her that she's really the younger, peppier sister of her former self.

In *Deuteronomy 8:7-9*, it is written: "a land of wheat and barley, and vines, and fig trees, and pomegranates, a land of olive oil and honey; a land wherein you shall eat bread without scarceness, you shall not lack anything in it...."
Grains, vegetables and fruits --this is what we can assume God wanted for us.

In *Ezekiel 4:9*, we even find a recipe for bread: "...take wheat, barley, beans, lentils, millet and emmer (oats). Put them into one vessel and bake them into bread."

We have met many people who maintain that personal circumstances make it impossible for them to change their diet. A man we know who has heart disease says he attends many business lunches and dinners. People will think he's sick. he says, if he doesn't eat the customary rubber meat, white cotton rolls stripped of their fiber, the salty, soggy, buttered vegetables and the sugary, gooey desserts.

One woman claims that she entertains often, and that her guests expect platters of cheeses and sweets.

How many times have we heard the saga of the grandfather who lived to be 97? You know, the nonagenarian who throughout his life stuffed himself with meat, fried foods, candy and ice cream. He also pushed aside anything on his plate that was green or yellow and smoked a corn cob pipe. Grandpa might have lucked out. Will you? It's your choice.

Of course, change is frightening. An anthropologist we know said diet is so culturally ingrained that many people can more easily be convinced to switch their religious beliefs than to alter their diet drastically. On holidays, we can almost smell the meals of celebrations past. The aromas of dinners served on the Sabbaths and Passovers waft across the years, even across the decades. We associate foods with events, with times when we felt protected and comforted. When we understand this, it is easier to change.

You have a choice. You can choose the grain-centered diet of *Genesis* for yourself, for your guests, for your precious family. You can enjoy the bounty of good health.

Your children can be more alert in school and free from frequent colds and infections. They can have the spunk that ejects them from a place in front of the television set and excites them to play ball, ride bikes, skate, draw, paint, sculpt, read and do chores. They are too dear to become the receptacles and conduits for the crunchy-munchy-crackle menu of junk and slurpy, sugary liquid that TV hucksters pitch to them.

To Your Health!

By the way, sugar suppresses the body's immune system for as long as 48 hours after you eat it. It can depress your mood, too. Try skipping it for a few weeks, and watch your attitude change.

You can encourage your synagogue to replace the sweet rolls and chocolate brownies at the *Oneg Shabbat* after the services with brown rice raisin pudding, oatmeal raisin cookies, carob brownies, fruit, nuts and popcorn.

You can offer your guests food that will build their health instead of food that will make them feel guilty.

Let's stop providing excuses for each other to indulge in harmful eating. Let's stop playing the food games. You know the ones: "I fixed this just for you." "One piece won't hurt anybody."

We have seen so much suffering in so many families, suffering which could have been avoided. We have paced a hospital corridor with a beautiful young widow-to-be whose husband was dying of cancer. Not long before, we had heard from him how his meat diet and cigarette smoking couldn't hurt him.

We have looked into the eyes of the teen-age boy whose father promised he would begin to lose weight as soon as he completed his next business deal. The fatal heart attack didn't wait.

We have steadied the quivering bodies of elderly parents in mourning their middle-aged daughter, a brilliant academician, dead of breast cancer.

You can choose not to put your loved ones through the ordeal of your illness and possible demise. We appeal to you. Care enough about yourself. Choose life!

Choose a return to the diet of *Genesis*, the diet of the ideal world. Be aware that, according to a number of Jewish scholars, including Rabbi Abraham Isaac ha-Kohen Kook (1865-1935), first Chief Rabbi of pre-state Israel, permission to eat meat was given only after the Flood, when God observed that human beings had become so corrupt that this concession was made.

There followed regulations over the eating of meat, which resulted in the Jewish dietary laws of *Kashruth*.

For our psychic as well as for our physical well-being, we must become aware of the realities of slaughter of animals for food. So-designated "humane slaughter"-- kosher and otherwise - is by its very nature a contradiction in terms. And the horrible method of slaughter does not even take into account the cruelty the animals suffer en route to the abattoir. Nor does it take into account that calves are snatched from their mothers at birth, placed in stalls in which they cannot even turn around, that baby chicks are debeaked and squashed into battery cages in which they are so crowded that the birds can barely move.

Can we be happy as human beings when our dinner plates are filled with the remains of animals who have lived in agony and died in fear? Can we nibble away at their flesh, their eggs, the milk and cheese that comes from horrors they have endured, and find peace within ourselves and with the universe?

Rabbi Kook insisted that peace on earth presupposes peace between people and animals.

His successor, the first Ashkenazi Chief Rabbi of the State of Israel, the late Rabbi Isaac Herzog (1888-1959), asserted that "Man's carnivorous nature is not taken for granted or praised in the fundamental teachings of Judaism. The rabbis of the Talmud told that men were vegetarians in earliest times, between Creation and the generation of Noah....

To Your Health!

"Judaism as a religion offers the option of eating animal flesh, and most Jews do, but in our own century.....a whole galaxy of central rabbinic and spiritual leaders.....has been affirming vegetarianism as the ultimate meaning of Jewish moral teaching. They have been proclaiming the autonomy of all living creatures as the value which our religious tradition must now teach to all of its believers......

"Jews will move increasingly to vegetarianism out of their own deepening knowledge of what their tradition commands as they understand it in this age."

The list of noted Jewish vegetarians includes two Nobel laureates in literature, Isaac Bashevis Singer and the late S.Y. Agnon (1888-1970), as well as the literary legend, Franz Kafka (1883-1924).

As we increase our reverence for all life, we increase reverence for ourselves, also, the reverence that can motivate us to take care of our bodies.

Jewish vegetarians join their non-Jewish peers in believing that vegetarianism can help alleviate world hunger. The world's land resources should be used to provide grains, vegetables and fruits for all instead of being ravaged to raise grain which is fed to animals who, in turn, are slaughtered to feed meat-eating human beings.

While the affluent consume animal products at breakfast, lunch and dinner, millions of the world's people starve. This is really ludicrous, when you consider that more than 80 percent of the corn and oats we grow is used to feed livestock, not people. More than half of the harvested farmland in the United States is used to grow food for livestock. One acre of land used to produce cattle feed will end up delivering 165 pounds of beef. That same acre could produce 20,000 pounds of potatoes, according to the Department of Agriculture. Our precious water resources, too, are evaporating, as half of the water we use in this country is used to irrigate land devoted to growing fodder for livestock.

To quench the appetite for meat, we have not only raped our own farmlands but have stripped the tropical rain forests of Central America and South America to convert them to pasture land for cattle.

We have the option of participating in the cruel and selfish system of animal food production or of cleansing ourselves of it.

In the *Apocrypha (30:16)*, Ben Sira said, "There is no wealth like health."

No wealth like health, yet we devour salty, fatty meals, swallow pills to calm our nerves, and maintain that we have no time to exercise, because we are trying to accumulate material wealth. We need a vegetarian diet to fuel our bodies properly and keep them from degenerative diseases. We need exercise to keep our muscles, including our heart muscles, toned. Exercise also keeps us calm, reduces anxiety and gives us confidence.

No time? Let's see.

Steve is a stockbroker. After a tense day of trading, he says good-bye to his colleagues, who head for cocktail lounges, where they wind down. Instead, Steve drives home. sheds his three-piece suit, dons his exercise clothes and walks. He says it's like a daily vacation that rejuvenates him.

Irene and David found it difficult to exercise regularly amid careers and caring for 6-year-old Michael and 18-month-old Abby. Now, after dinner, instead of plopping down in front of the TV, the family goes walking. Abby is pushed in her stroller,

Michael sometimes rides a small, two-wheeler. The walks last from 30 minutes to an hour. The family is not only healthier but closer.

Karen is single and lives in a large Eastern city. The irregular hours demanded by her position as a merchandising executive make it hard for her to join a buddy group of walkers or runners. Karen's answer is an exercise bicycle. She pedals 20 miles while listening to jazz or, occasionally, watching a sitcom.

Rena is an attorney in her 30s. Three times a week she spends her lunch breaks playing racquetball. After her workout, she munches on a whole-grain sandwich, filled with a bean spread and heaped with sprouts. Her favorite beverage is naturally-carbonated water spiked with fruit juice. The other two lunches are reserved for power meal meetings. Sunday mornings, she hikes with an environmental group.

The Goldsteins have four children, two from Don's former marriage, one from Alicia's and one child from their union. They play nightly games of catch during the summer and have table tennis sessions during the winter to help cement their family identity. Last year, they added weekly hikes to the roster of activities. Family members take turns choosing trails within a 45-minute drive from their home.

Three times a day, our dear friend, Kay, walks Kiska, the cuddly, winsome Malamute she adopted from the S.P.C.A. eight years ago. A musician and painter, Kay, who turned 88 this year, just had an art studio built in her home.

Rabbi Mordecai M. Kaplan, the founder of the Jewish Reconstructionist movement who passed away in 1983 at the age of 102, for decades walked daily to and from his home in New York, at 104th Street and Central Park West, and the Society for the Advancement of Judaism at 86th Street and Central Park West.

In addition to our regular exercises of running, walking and bicycling, we have replaced cocktail time with the dog-walk for our "happy hour." Every night, we take our dogs, Adam and Dodi, on a walk around our townhouse complex. We are usually joined by other friends with and without their own dogs. For several years, until his death, we also had as a walking companion Herman, a stray, tabby cat who adopted our friend and neighbor, Lois. Herman heeled as well as all of the dogs in the parade, which sometimes has as many as a dozen participants.

So, pick your sport: running (Betty's favorite), walking (Sid's. He alternates five-mile walks with 20-mile rides on the exercise bike), tennis, dancing, hiking, swimming -- and enjoy. Let your body tingle with exhilaration.

One man we know -- we'll call him Ed -- jokes that the glass he lifts every night is his form of exercise. There's no comedy here. Ed comes home from a day as a top officer of a major corporation and immediately guzzles two cocktails. This is chased with a gourmet dinner accompanied by at least three glasses of wine. Ed maintains he doesn't need the alcohol. He would do fine without it. He just enjoys it. He never has to test his theory, because he's never stranded anywhere where the drinks aren't flowing.

Jews are not teetotalers. Moderate amounts of wine have been used to sanctify the Sabbath and festivals. Consumed in such small quantities and only on special occasions in the warm, secure comfort of the home, there was no threat to the health of the body or the mind. Today, the rate of alcoholism among Jews competes with that of society at large. Please check your consumption. If you need help, seek out a support group.

Similarly, if you have been seduced by drugs, we beseech you to seek treatment. Let your family know that you need help and that you need their support.

Love yourself enough not to pollute your body with smoke. If you're hooked on nicotine, you can choose to stop. You can join a stop-smoking group or go to a clinic. The key is sticking to your commitment. Smoking is considered the single greatest health risk. Your body deserves to be smoke-free.

The bottom line to changing to a healthy life style is your commitment. The ultimate power to the healthiest you possible lies within you.

You are a valuable being who deserves care and nurturing. There is only one of you. Sanctify your uniqueness. Remember, you can choose health. You can choose to eat the vegetarian, grain-based diet recommended in *Genesis*. You can choose to exercise. You can choose to limit your alcohol consumption. You can choose to stub out your cigarette habit and not to pop pills.

You can look at yourself and decide that you deserve to have only good things enter your body and good things happen to your body. The more you take care of yourself, the better you'll feel, and the more you'll like yourself. The more you like yourself, the better care you'll take.

"... and if not now, when?" You can choose life. Please do!

6

The Wonder of Nature

"In the whole realm of nature there is nothing purposeless, trivial or unnecessary."
>   Maimonides (1135-1204), *Guide for the Perplexed*

Char would love to live in a house. She grew up in one in the Midwest, a three-bedroom-plus-den ranch house with a big backyard where she and her brother and sister and their friends could play badminton, croquet and touch football, run under sprinklers in the summer and build snowmen in the winter. They would picnic under the apple trees and play games of retrieve the ball with Princess and Asta and Skipper, the family dogs. Most of all, she remembers the vegetable garden.

Widowed now, and with two young children to raise, Char says buying a house is about as realistic for her as the purchase of a Manhattan office tower would be. Child care gobbles up a hefty chunk of her take-home pay in a city where real estate prices continue to leap. She considers herself lucky to have managed a two-bedroom condo in a quiet suburb.

What she did with that condo! Enter the living room. To create a view where none existed (except for that of the Abramson's living room across the court), Char hung baskets of bushy grape ivy. Split-leaf philodendrons sit courting the sun in 18-inch clay pots on the floor. Baskets of pine cones decorate table tops. Driftwood, small branches and twigs peek out from ceramic vases. In the dining room/den, pots of the grape ivy are nestled in wrought iron plant holders attached to the wall.

The room, shared by Nessa, 8, and Susie, 5, has a shelf garden, where the girls raise their own plants, take cuttings, root them in water and plant them in every conceivable container from cans to mugs. Baskets of shells and rocks and pebbles are at home with the girls' books and games and art supplies.

Char's own bedroom/office is home for two palm trees.

Their condo kitchen has become an indoor farm with the herb garden on the window sill and the mung beans, azuki beans, lentils and alfalfa sprouting in the jars that line one side of the counter top. Sprigs of dried basil, rosemary and oregano hang from the ceiling, their aroma wafting through the home.

Char, Nessa and Susie feel a strong involvement with nature here. So does Pinkus, the 12-pound poodle terrier dog they adopted from an animal rescue group. His companionship and antics add to the wonders of nature that fill this special home.

Barry, a partner in a large accounting firm, spends a typical day meeting with anxious clients, solving staff problems and analyzing new business regulations and tax laws. His world of figures and computers, meetings and training sessions is happily interrupted when he tends to his office garden.

A backyard gardener who for years had relished getting his hands dirty as he dug, sowed, seeded, planted, watered, weeded and fertilized trees, shrubs and flowers and vegetables, Barry realized that he could experience during the work day some of the calm he felt in his garden.

He unloaded on the floor of his office four ficus benjamina trees in 18-inch ceramic containers, creating a small forest. On the window sill in front of the trees, he placed four African violets, two Norsemen and two Dolly Dimples, all basking in a southern exposure. He set up a small table under a window that has a northern exposure, perfect for the pots of peperomia he set upon it.

Barry has noticed that the minor annoyances which used to goad him during the day hardly bother him as he reduces stress by gazing at his plants, watering them, misting their leaves, snipping them as needed.

The only drawback to this arrangement is that everyone wants to meet in his office. The other partners and junior accountants say it just feels good in that room.

Helene is a social worker whose case load is heavy with abused children. Hers is a constant struggle of proving maltreatment, confronting angry and defensive parents, shuttling the children to safety, connecting with hospital nurses and doctors, soothing the emotional pain of the traumatized youngsters, untying the knots of government bureaucracies and testifying in court.

She's watched many of her colleagues burn out from being wrung through the emotional wringer. Helene doesn't want that to happen to her. She's discovered that she is better able to help children when she is calm.

Her relief comes in the form of daily "vacation outings," as she calls them. Almost every workday, she eats lunch in a pocket park near her office. She lets the trees fan her with their swaying branches. She's a gleeful audience for the squirrels, who scurry and romp across the grass and scoot up the trees.

When the weather is bad, she sits in her car by the park and munches away, as she watches the rain fall on the grass and trees. When her schedule makes the lunch outing impossible, she takes an afternoon snack break with nature.

As she drives to the next destination where trouble might be brewing, Helene plays tapes of ocean waves and waterfalls. Sometimes, she plays music inspired by nature themes.

Is it any surprise that studies conducted at major universities have indicated that even brief exposure to nature significantly reduces stress? A Texas A & M University study reports that patients who had access to views of greenery left the hospital an average of a day earlier than patients who looked out at brick or concrete walls. Is it any wonder that flowers and plants are welcomed gifts to people who are hospitalized?

"Trees were created for people's companionship."
Genesis Rabbah (Midrash) 13:2

Take a few moments later today -- at the latest, tomorrow -- and really look at a tree. Look at its trunk, the designs of the bark. Watch, as some of the branches dance to the caress of the breeze. Can you spot a butterfly fluttering among the leaves? Are there chirping birds perched on the limbs or branches? Are the leaves all the exact same shade of green? Study the veins of the leaves. What variations can you spot? Are the roots large, and do they reach out over the cracks they make in the earth?

Do you realize, as you gaze upon this glory, that the tree will never look exactly like this again? Some leaves will fall. Others will be born. The bark will peel. Shadows will play in different ways. Shift your gaze with the changing choreography.

"The person who sees a tree in bloom shall pronounce a benediction."   adapted from *Berakhot (Talmud) 43b*

When we enjoy any plant, we tend to feel part of the entire cosmos. The wonders of life abound in the greenery of the trees and shrubs, in the riot of color of the flowers.

Nature makes us feel blissful, part of the entire picture of life.

Animals make us feel close to nature. They force us to focus on the moment. Human beings of all ages have been made happy by the cheer of loving animals. Studies have proved that petting a dog or cat can even lower one's blood pressure. Would you want to argue with the dog or cat who makes you feel like the finest person who ever lived, the companion animal whose greatest moment of joy is when you return home?

Our relationships with our dogs, Adam and Dodi, bring out our sense of play, our interaction with nature, our ability to communicate with another species. These beloved friends emulate the best we seek in relationships with human beings: love, loyalty and honesty.

Dodi, the shepherd mix, has taught us what real concentration is. A superb tennis ball catcher, his eye doesn't leave the sphere for a split second when he's readying to catch a fly ball.

Front paws braced in front of him on the floor, his back arched so that his hind legs are straight up, ears perked, mouth ready to open wide when the ball goes into the air, he leaps high and opens his mouth just as the sphere is about to descend.

Dodi wakes up each morning in a state of jubilation over the prospect of playing ball and the other adventures the day might present.

Last year, a minor skin infection forced Dodi to wear an Elizabethan collar that prevented him from biting his underside. "He's probably not going to like this," said the veterinarian, as he showed us how to adjust the cumbersome contraption.

Dodi never complained. He found new ways of ducking to catch the ball without allowing the collar to become a hindrance. He tested several sleeping positions until he found one that agreed with him. He asked for help only in being properly positioned over his food bowl. He walked outside with his tail up, like the proud and joyful dog he is.

Adam is a more serious fellow. Our friend, Linda, says he carries his responsibiities on his shoulders. Actually he carries a lot of them in his mouth. A regal-looking Labrador mix, he is happiest when he carries things upstairs for us. Jackets, sweat shirts, magazines, beach towels, even canvas brief cases, all are carried by Adam, the consummate bellhop.

Adam also talks a lot, especially when a guest dares to sit, unwittingly, on the green couch in our playroom, the one couch on which Adam and Dodi are allowed. This situation is usually remedied when the guest moves to the left side of the couch, permitting our 75-pound protector to leap up, lie down and curl up with his big head snuggled on the lap of the guest.

"Various philosophers and religious leaders tried to convince their disciples and followers that animals are nothing more than machines without a soul, without feelings. However, anyone who has ever lived with an animal.....knows that this theory is a brazen lie, invented to justify cruelty,"
Isaac Bashevis Singer (1904),
1978 Nobel Prize laureate for Literature

The Friends of Animals Foundation in Los Angeles reported the passing at 15 years of Billy. Billy was a Labrador mix who had shared his affection for nine years with the elderly, the crippled and the lonely in nursing homes as well as in the "Pet

Therapy" program of an area medical center.

Billy's affections were unconfined. He gave of his love freely, even if the hands that reached out to pet him trembled. Sometimes, Billy had to be lifted up to comfort a bedridden patient; no matter. The passing of the only visitor that came regularly to brighten otherwise lonely Sunday afternoons at the nursing homes was devastating.

According to the patients, Billy was "the only source of love in a world that had, otherwise, forgotten them."

A companion animal will bring you untold joy, love and devotion, as well as hours of entertainment.

But -- we beseech you! -- please do not adopt a dog or cat unless you're ready to make a major commitment for as long as a decade and a half, depending upon the age of the animal. Your companion animal is totally dependent upon you. You are the difference between hunger and satiation, between thirst and its quenching, between loneliness and companionship for him or her. We're talking about beings who feel hunger, thirst, pain, fear, loneliness. They mourn, they sulk, they kibbitz.

Proper veterinary care must be provided. And in a society where as many as 20 million puppies, kittens, dogs and cats are killed each year in animal shelters, we urge you to have your friend spayed or neutered. Even if you manage the almost impossible task of finding good homes for all of your pet's offspring, you are just taking away those homes from other animals who need them to live. It's like a life-and-death game of musical chairs for pets. Too many animals for too few available homes.

If you decide that adopting a companion animal will work for you and the animal, please go to an animal shelter or rescue group.

The Wonder of Nature

Consider adopting an older animal.

We know you can't take them all home. But, remember, Judaism believes that if you save one life it's as if you saved the entire world.

If you would like the joy that a cat or dog can bring but can't take on the responsibility, enjoy a friend's companion or volunteer at a shelter. Offer to walk the dog of an elderly neighbor, or feed and play with a neighbor's cat while your neighbor takes a week-end trip. Rescue groups desperately need volunteers to walk, pet and play with homeless animals.

Judaism has a tradition of kindness to animals. It is set forth very explicitly in the concept of *tsa'ar ba'alay hayyim*, concern over "the pain of living creatures."

"Had the Torah not been given to us," the *Talmud* observes, "we would have learned modesty from cats, honest activity from ants, purity from doves and gallantry from roosters." *(Eruvin 100b)*

Judaism is traditionally opposed to hunting and fishing. "It is not the way of the children of Abraham, Isaac and Jacob," declared one sage.

"...I will make a covenant for them with the beasts of the field, the birds of the air, and the creeping things of the ground; I shall also banish bow, sword and war from the land. Thus I will let them lie down in safety."

Hosea 2:20

Judaism's respect for nature is celebrated throughout the year.

In the fall, just after the Jewish New Year, comes Sukkot, the fall harvest festival. It is observed in the outdoors in a *sukkah*, a booth put together in remembrance of the overnight lean-tos in which the Israelites rested on their journey from Egypt to the Promised Land. Jews use a palm branch, a citron, a myrtle sprig and willows of the brook in part of the Sukkot ritual.

In January comes Tu BiShvat, or Hamisha Asar BiShvat, the 15th day of the Hebrew month of Shvat. This is the "New Year of the Trees," sometimes called the Jewish Arbor Day. In the state of Israel, school children plant trees on this day.

Spring welcomes Passover, the "Festival of Springtime." We've taken Passover season hikes through Topanga Canyon in the Santa Monica Mountains. There, we walked through fields of poppies that stretched so far we felt as if they were falling off the end of the earth. We spent one memorable Passover seder with friends in the Mojave desert, with only the cactus and the rocks and the arid soil -- a true wilderness experience to recall the Exodus.

Shavuot, the spring harvest festival, comes in June. It is called the "Festival of the First Fruits," because, in Bible days, Israelites journeyed to the Temple in Jerusalem to present the first fruits of the late spring harvest.

The splendor of nature is spread out for you to protect and enjoy. Allow its constant renewal of life to enthrall you and boost your happiness quotient. It is a constant renewal of life that helps us understand life's sanctity.

Try to take day trips to the glorious treasures in your area: the mountains, the desert, the ocean, the prairie, the forest. A few hours in any one of these places can make you feel as if you've been away for days.

Visit parks and public gardens.

Plant a garden. Feel the dirt. Your garden can take up an acre of land or just your kitchen window sill.

The Wonder of Nature

Start a sprout garden in that kitchen. Sprinkle your harvest on your salads.

Festoon your home with nature's gifts: rocks, pebbles, beach glass, driftwood, twigs, pine cones.

Consider the sky. The cloud formations. What do you see? Step out and look at the stars, at the constellations, the moon.

Delight in the sunset. Set your alarm and watch the sunrise.

Notice the grass growing between the cracks of the sidewalk.

Enjoy the lavishly-planted window boxes growing in crowded cities.

Smell the flowers. Tumble on the lawn!

Follow the rainbow! Feel the morning dew.

Lift your face up to catch the mist and the drizzle and the snowflakes!

7

There's A World Out There

"The wise store up knowledge."

Proverbs 10:14

Think about your children and grandchildren, your nieces, nephews, young friends and neighbors. Aren't you consistently amazed by their latest observation, their witty statements, the new words they use and the information they pick up and often share with you?

So many lucky kids get absorbed in the wonders of the world, in everything from dinosaurs and sailing ships to stars and computers.

You don't have to be a kid to experience this sense of ongoing discovery and wonder. You can have a super-terrific adulthood when you open yourself up to learning.

The question our mothers asked us when we came home from school,"What did you learn today?" is one that can be asked of us throughout our lives.

For Jews, learning has been one of the main purposes of living. "He who acquires wisdom is his own best friend. He preserves understanding and attains happiness." *Proverbs 19:8*

People of all ages are finding the words of *Proverbs* to be relevant for them. They are becoming interested and interesting, more self-assured and happier as they pursue information and ideas that no one can take away from them.

Clare and Ron have been married for 19 years. They are the parents of two teen-agers and have demanding careers. They love the kids, and they love their jobs, but pressures of work and family life brought tension into the marriage. A sharp counselor said they needed to spend more time together. These were two people who just about had to pencil an evening alone into their respective calendars. Even when it came to exercise, she went to an aerobics class, while he was smashing away on a squash court.

They recalled how they had first met in a college history course. Now, they attend class together at University Extension. Last spring, they studied Shakepeare. This fall, it's the Structure of the Symphony. One night a week is theirs. They have dinner, attend class and after class they go out for a snack or take a walk when the weather is nice. Ron still thinks Clare is the loveliest coed on campus. And they still haven't broken the habit of slipping notes to each other, when the instructor isn't looking.

Frieda is a 68-year-old widow who takes an oil painting class in the adult education program of the local high school. That's on Monday nights. Tuesday nights are reserved for her Introduction to Acting class. Frieda would like to sign up for more classes, but she doesn't have the time. She volunteers at a hospital on Thursdays, and she spends two hours on Wednesdays at the library, teaching a 54-year-old woman how to read through the library's literacy project.

Don't try to see her on Thursday nights. That's when Frieda alternates cooking dinner with two other friends. Each cooks for all three of them one Thursday night a month. On the fourth Thursday night, they eat out. They've been enjoying their Thursday nights for four and a half years. Friday night is temple night.

Frieda's children line her up two and three weeks ahead to see her. And, if they want to see her on Sundays, they had better plan on a trip to a museum or an afternoon concert. That is Frieda's culture day.

Molly was in the doldrums at work. Exhausted by the time she left the office, it was all she could do to get home, grab something to eat and drop down in front of the TV. When a friend suggested they sign up for classes at the local community college, Molly balked that she didn't have the time.

When Molly flipped on the TV, she joined millions of Americans who turn over the precious hours of their lives to trite, recycled scripts, titillating displays of scantily-clad bodies, acts of violence, pseudo-journalistic talk shows whose producers vie to outsensationalize one another.

In between all of this programming, designed to snare unthinking audiences onto the charts of cost per thousands, our homes are opened to hawkers of every conceivable commodity that promises to make us socially acceptable and relieve our pain.

The average American spends four hours and 20 minutes a day in front of the television set. That's more than 30 hours a week. That means more than one entire day of a person's week is devoted to television. The set is on in the average home seven hours and 10 minutes a day, according to the A.C. Nielsen rating service. Author Marie Winn in her book, *The Plug-In Drug*, contends that watching TV is addictive. Many people sit and watch TV because it's easy, and it numbs you.

"More than all that you guard, guard your mind. For it is the source of life."

Proverbs 4:23

Molly turned off her TV. She stopped being a spectator of life and became a liver of life.

She attends community college classes twice a week. Studying 20th Century American Literature and Art Appreciation has revolutionized her life. She's not only busy attending classes but reading great novels and preparing for discussions. She meets other students for dinner before class. After the Lit group, Molly joins a half-dozen other students who go to a coffee shop or someone's house to discuss what the professor said in the lecture.

Molly has gotten into the habit of visiting art museums and galleries. And she's planning a trip to California's Monterey Peninsula to explore close-up the country that inspired some of her favorite authors: John Steinbeck, Sinclair Lewis and Robinson Jeffers. She's grown to love Jeffers' poetry. She still watches TV a few hours a week but very selectively. She loves that front-row seat to a finely-produced British drama.

People of all ages are students once again, earning degrees or just taking courses that interest them. The thing to do is decide where your interests lie and do what's right for you. You can learn to:
• study for your Bat or Bar Mitzvah,
• debate all the isms of Judaism,
• read Camus in the original French,
• fire pots,
• fix your own car,
• write short stories,
• master computers,
• paint with water colors,
• make creative photographs,

• play the flute.

You can learn about astronomy, archaeology, anthropology, botany, history, journalism, political science, literature, theatre, film history, sociology and theology.

You can join classes at community colleges, universities, synagogues, adult schools, park district facilities, community centers, senior centers and women's centers Remember, you can earn a degree or study a subject out of interest. You can attend traditional classes, seminars or workshops.

Whichever you choose, before you will lie an authentic fountain of youth!

Betty has had as students in her journalism classes a 60-year-old physician who wanted to learn how to write a news story and find out how newspapers worked, and a bright-eyed and feisty 70-year-old woman en route to earning a bachelor's degree, together with scores of 18-year-olds, 26-year-olds, 49 year-olds and everyone in between, all involved with each other, sharing their experiences and their ambitions, all involved in learning.

There's an added bonus to all this schooling. Do you remember how much fun it was to
buy school supplies?
run your hand across the new tablet of lined paper?
have pencils with brand new erasers?
gather brightly-colored pens and pencils for underlining?
pile all the goodies on top of each other?
Well, go for it! Don't let the kids have all the fun.

Learn, also, by reading. Dive into subjects. Take an author, read her biography, and then read her novels. Make friends with your library. Rummage through used book stores. A book can transport you to another time, another place.

Read on breaks. Read while you're waiting for the rice to boil. Read yourself to sleep. Read in the park. Read in the motel room. Read in the bathroom.

Treat yourself to museums, historical societies and tours of Victorian houses. Explore . . . discover . . . and get excited!

8

The Joy of Creativity

"To live means to create."
> Rabbi Milton Steinberg (1903-1950),
> *A Partisan Guide, 1945*

When Sheila swishes the brush through the dollop of paint on her palette and with broad strokes applies color to her latest canvas, she is immersed in the moment. All her woes seem to fade as her picture takes on life.

Kenneth sits at his computer and pours his joys, frustrations and dreams into his poetry. Sometimes his work is whimsical, when he writes birthday sonnets for lucky friends and relatives.

Martin and Blanche string wooden, glass and paper-mache beads into necklaces and bracelets.

Jean fills loose-leaf notebooks with reams of short stories she writes late at night when everyone else in the house is asleep.

Sheila, Kenneth, Martin, Blanche and Jean have all discovered that by expressing themselves in creative ways they are building confidence and reducing stress, as they are better able to live for the moment.

Everything you create will be a tangible extension of yourself.

You can sketch, write poetry, fire pots, paint, do needlepoint, take photographs, shoot videos, write short stories, compose songs, paint rocks, whittle wood, make cork bulletin boards or choreograph dances just for you.

Express yourself: your dreams, your frustrations, your joys, snatches of your life, your interpretation of the world.

Go ahead! Make a statement!

9

Making Friends

Get yourself a companion," is advice offered in the post-Biblical *Ethics of the Fathers*, one of Judaism's basic texts.

You are entitled to develop friendships, to bask in the warmth of secure and supportive relationships.

How lonely, cold and alienating the world must sometimes seem. How shut out and abandoned we can feel, even when we are in the company of others.

How sorrowful and agonizing can be the pain crying out from a solitary heart.

There are choices to be made whether we have relationships with others, just as there are choices about the nature of those relationships. Our attitudes and actions will be the determining factors whether we are to be throttled by relatives, co-workers and friends or thrive from knowing them and being with them.

Judaism does not want us to be alone. It is a religion that encourages social interaction. Even when we pray, Jews do so collectively, not individually and alone. The presence of a *minyan*, a quorum of ten, is required to validate a worship service.

"Do not keep aloof from the community," said Hillel, one of the formulators of Judaism.

You deserve to make friends, to feel included, to share experiences with others. The choices we make about what friendship is, our treatment of others and our choices about our attitudes can determine what role friendship plays in our lives.

Some people try to make friends with those whom they consider the right people. They seek out those who will do them the most good at work, the guy who can get them into the country club, the hot business connection, the leader of the in-crowd. Relationships should revolve around mutual respect, not use of one person by another.

Josh and Melanie knew that their steel-and-glass house designed by a prominent architect would launch their social position in the northern Chicago suburb. Josh carefully played his deck of people at the law firm, cozying up to the senior partners and darting out of the paths of those he labeled as losers. Melanie planned gourmet dinners for the legal brahmins in Josh's firm and made sure to lunch with their wives. When she discovered that one of the wives was a golfer, Melanie hired a golf pro to give her lessons. She learned to tee off to a respectable score, making sure never to beat the partner's wife. Josh calculated that a country club membership would help bring new clients to the firm. So, Melanie investigated who sat on the membership committee of the club and went to work. "We're in!" she proclaimed at dinner.

Their scheme worked. Josh recruited clients; Melanie continued to cook gourmet dinners; they were invited to the best theme parties; the money flowed. But Josh and Melanie were dying inside. They had no one to talk to, no one with whom to share simple things. Josh suffered a heart attack, and no one came to the hospital to visit. They had no friends.

Aaron learned about friendship in college. When he was a junior, he got in with Tom, Lance and Rog, who loved to party. One week-end during mid-terms, Aaron faced studying for back-to-back exams scheduled for Monday, one in philosophy, the other in chemistry. A major term paper for English literature was due Tuesday. The guys urged him to cool it. He needed a break. Too much studying would make him actually fail, Lance argued.

Aaron allowed himself to ditch the books for the fun. He flunked the chemistry mid-term and sank low enough in philosophy to kill his chance for an A or B. The lit paper was turned in late, and his grade plummeted. He bumped into an old high school chum, T.J., who over lunch listened to Aaron's defense of how his friends had meant well. "Good friends want you to succeed and not be stressed," said T.J. "Were these guys going to support you, if you flunked out of college?"

Friends care about you. Friends are happy to listen to your problems; they give advice when asked; they don't tear you down.

Friends do not encourage you to spill your guts out about how terrible your family is. It's one thing for someone to be a confidant during times of stress, another for someone to derive pleasure from your difficulties and emotional pain. Jealousy doesn't fare well in friendship; neither do sarcasm nor defensiveness.

Friends refrain from gossiping. "As you speak no slander, so listen to none, for if it had no hearers, it would have no bearers." said Eliezer ben Samuel ha-Levi, 14th century author of an ethical will. Yet some relationships are based on tearing down of third parties.

81

Making Friends

The *Ethics of the Fathers* urges that we "Meet every person with a friendly greeting." What an elegant suggestion for making friends, being friendly, greeting people with a smile, showing you're happy to see them.

This is a positive idea, the opposite of the "I dare you to take me on" greeting foisted upon us by people like Muriel.

Muriel would say hello to the other committee members at the local library fund-raising meetings, but she never added a smile to her hello and never put a lilt in her voice. She was quick to point out mistakes that other committee members made but offered no compliments. She typically wore a scowl and looked as if she had just swallowed a sourdrop.

Wish a good day to Cora, and you may be in for a verbal flogging. "I hurt my back and had to stay in the house for two weeks. Do you think anyone came to see me? Do you think anyone cared? I could drop dead, and no one would care." Cora forgets to mention that she never calls anyone to inquire about their good and welfare.

Brenda does a superb job of chasing friends away. She is highly intelligent and a punchy conversationalist; but watch out when she gets on the defensive. Witness her taunting reaction to a phone call that didn't come just when she would have liked. "It's about time. I thought there would be another solar eclipse, before you would pick up the phone."

We all know people who make others uncomfortable. Through their conscious or unconscious choices, they make people want to stay clear of them. We work with these people, have them as neighbors, attend classes with them, encounter them in business; often, we are related to them. They are quick to point out our faults. They challenge others to make them smile in response to their grumpy attitudes. They blow up small problems into issues they would like to see covered on the 6

82

o'clock news. They are bored by life. They don't like themselves very much, so they're not sure how to like you.

And they whack us with their verbal onslaughts.

Such personalities see themselves as perpetual victims, and, sure enough, their attitude of self-victimization eventually becomes self-fulfilling.

If you want to have friends, smile, be happy to see people, display an interest in what's happening to them. Everyone has a story. Dig it out. People love to talk about themselves. People want to be around people who are interested in them. When acquaintances phone, tell them it is terrific to hear from them. Make them look forward to talking to you, not dread it. Understand that if someone else is in a funk, you shouldn't take it personally,

People who are genuinely interested in others find they have a care-net waiting for them, if they run into trouble.

Choose the kind word, not the cutting remark.

"Pleasant words are like a honeycomb, sweet to the palate and a cure for the body," we are reminded in *Proverbs 16:24.*

Jeff was out walking one night, when he spotted a neighbor making his rounds. There had appeared in the newspaper that morning an article about the neighbor's son, who was facing serious difficulty in his attempt to be re-elected to the local school board. Jeff almost said, "What's this about Chuck's problem?" But he caught himself, realizing that his neighbor need respite. He was out to walk, to relax a bit, to find relief from his family's heavy, tension-packed involvement in the son's campaign. Jeff anticipated his neighbor's need and greeted him with, "Good evening. It's good to see you."

Making Friends

When you're in a good mood, and someone asks you how you are, respond with "wonderful" or "terrific." If you say it often enough, you'll feel terrific more often. That makes the other person feel as if he or she has done something wonderful and that he or she is wonderful. Others will love to be around you.

Be a builder-upper, not a tearer-downer. If someone asks for advice or your opinion, by all means give it. But don't feel you're obligated to tell your friends that they're too fat or that their outfit isn't stylish. Most people know their own problems. They don't need to have them pointed out. Let them know that you think they're great, if they are. Tell them you appreciate something they did or said. All the awards, all the trophies, all the plaques in the world can't equal the informal nice words we hear from others.

We derive riches from friends of all ages and all walks of life. It is sad to see so many people segregate their friendships into niches. One couple we knew spent all of their social time with other couples who were their age. Several divorces occurred in the group, leaving the new singles isolated because they no longer fit in. We grow from enjoying a variety of people in our lives. If you have friends in their 80s, 90s and 100s, you are blessed with their experience and wisdom.

Children make great friends, too. Meagan, now 10, has taught us how to play all kinds of games, how to find the best drinking fountains at Disneyland and how to search for leaf prints in the cement. Kids are great for unfolding secrets of the universe and explaining them in language everyone can understand.

"Make not those who live under your roof dread your presence." cautioned Eliezer ben Isaac of Worms, 11th century sage.

Create a friendly atmosphere in your home. Don't devote the precious days you have with your loved ones to alienating them and making them feel worthless.

We are acquainted with a family in which the father is an esteemed university administrator and the mother, who has a master's degree in history, is active in community affairs. They have three children. The eldest is doing postgraduate work in physics. One, a high school sophomore, is an honors student. The middle son, a high school senior, doesn't like school, although he earns passing grades. He spends a lot of time writing folk music, playing baseball and basketball. He loves to fix cars and wants to attend a trade school in order to be an auto mechanic He has a job at a foreign car repair shop. He also works at a youth center, where he coaches baseball.

"How did I ever bear a misfit like you?" his mother complains in his presence.

If you are blessed with a husband or wife and children, caress the moments you have with them.

Friendship is especially important in these times, when many people are unmarried and don't have family living nearby. Forty percent of all adults in the United States live alone.

Good friends can form extended families and celebrate birthdays and holidays together. Travel, meals and outings can be shared. Support systems can be built.

Friendships usually begin with common interests. We can meet friends at work, in the neighborhood, at school, at synagogue or church, working for causes, at hobby groups, wherever people gather.

Sometimes, we experience moments of bonding with people we're unlikely to meet again. These moments pepper the long-standing relationships we build with others. We remember rock-hounding around Parker, Arizona, about 15 years ago, when we struck up a conversation with a bristly-faced codger who told us about the area, offered us coffee and presented us with two small crystals he had found.

Some people enjoy having a variety of friends. Others are content to have one or two close companions. Pursue whatever works for you. There are many wonderful people. You are one of them! Let the wonderful stuff inside of you out. There are good people who want, need and deserve your friendship.

And, what if you are rejected? You will come to understand that people who reject you are afraid to let go of the little, if any, warmth they feel. They do not realize that the more love you show the more you get. Love and friendship are not finite reserves. They are continually renewed as they are used. Feel sorry for those who appear self-satisfied and unfriendly.

Several years ago, we attended religious services at a large suburban congregation. A sad-faced man walked around wearing a badge that read, "Ask me about membership." He was so glum and unfriendly that the membership roll surely wasn't cranked up that night. Someone so unsure of his own self-worth was in a weak position to let prospective members know how they would be valued in the synagogue. It is so easy to be hurt by people like this. Please remember, we can't change others, but we can change our reactions to them.

Spread joy! Smile! Perk up someone's day with a happy thought. Call old friends and tell them you just want to hear the sound of their voice. Write a letter to someone you haven't seen in years. Don't worry about style. Just jot down notes. Provide them with details of a day in your life: the book you read, a meal you enjoyed, a lecture you heard, the music that soothed you, the flowers that bloomed. Tell them you miss them.

Don't wait until you can host an elaborate dinner party. Call up a few people you really like and invite them over for baked potatoes, salad, whole grain bread and fresh fruit. Tell them to wear jeans and t-shirts and be ready to relax.

Extend friendship, caring love, support and joy.

10

Fun and Joy

"...Let them attain joy and gladness,
While sorrow and sighing flee."

Isaiah 51:11

Your life should be filled with joy.

Other people can tell you jokes, tease you, tickle your spirits.
They can dance with you, sing with you and play with you. But
the person who has the prime role of concocting fun in your life
is you.

"Pleasant sounds, sights and smells put one in good spirits,"
says the *Talmud*.

Thanks to modern electronic technology, via broadcast, rec-
ords, cassettes and compact discs, we can invite singers and
instrumentalists, living and dead, into our homes. We can
create whatever musical environment we seek at the moment,
as we select from classical, jazz, show, folk, rock and country.

We can have fun playing music. Even those of us who never
learned to read notes and count measures can rattle maracas,
shake tambourines and click castanets. We can clap our
hands, snap our fingers and tap our toes. And if you've been

89

hankering to play an instrument, you can learn.

How music can lift the spirit! Check out concerts and recitals in your community. There are musical choices for every pocketbook. You may be enthralled occupying an orchestra seat in an impressive philharmonic auditorium. And you may have a memorable experience sitting on the gym risers at a school band concert.

Dance! Dance at parties, at weddings, at Bar Mitzvahs, at home. Dance with a group. Dance with a partner. Dance by yourself. Whirl and swirl and twirl and reach for the stars. Try folk dancing. Try square dancing. Try being Martha Graham or Mikhail Baryshnikov and choreograph your own interpretive dances in your bedroom or living room. Why not put on some tap shoes and go for it?

Sing! Sing in the shower, in the garden, in the kitchen, in the car. Whistle, hum, warble. Don't worry whether audiences would pay $50 a seat to hear you croon. On-key or off-key, sing for yourself. Sing, because you're alive.

Laugh! Roar, chuckle, guffaw. Rent Marx Brothers' movies. Watch re-runs of *I Love Lucy*. Check out the cartoons in newspapers and magazines.

Humor has always played a significant role in Jewish life. Some people who have had only a superficial acquaintance with Judaism have a mistaken view of Jewish culture as being dour and humorless. Not so at all!

Indeed, one of the seven basic benedictions in the Jewish marriage ceremony refers to "the voice of gladness and the voice of joy," equating them with the the voices of the bridegroom and of the bride, and speaks of God as the Creator of joy and gladness.

A Jewish wedding in an earlier age almost always had in attendance a *badchen,* a combination of wedding jester and master of ceremonies, who enlivened the festivities with his patter. Perhaps he was a forerunner of the *tummler* at Jewish resorts in the Catskill mountains, the "borscht belt," who served to keep things and people moving.

There is even an entire Jewish holiday devoted to fun. Purim, usually observed in March, commemorates the escape of the Jews of Persia from annihilation. It has been celebrated with carnivals, door-to-door "trick or treat" visitations and street theatre.

It's no accident and no surprise, then, to find that, in the Western world, Jews constitute a majority of the comedians and writers of comedy material. Sometimes, it has been, to use the Yiddish phrase, *lachter mit yashtcherkes,* laughter with tears, but laughter is indigenous to the Jewish soul.

Play! Play roly-poly with a gurgling baby. Play peek-a-boo. Frolic with a gleeful toddler. Play catch with your dog. Play string games with your cat. Play Frisbee. Play Ping-Pong. Skip rope. Bounce a ball. Shoot pool. Spin a Hula Hoop. Play board games. Play card games. Pitch your crumpled papers into the wastebasket. Solve puzzles. The choice is yours.

Celebrate! Celebrate birthdays, anniversaries and gradu-ations -- and anything else you can think of. Have picnics and parties and sing-alongs. Keep them simple, so you can have them often. Ask for poems in lieu of gifts. Which birthday or anniversary are you waiting to celebrate? We can be sure only of today's. It's your birthday, and you're by yourself? Treat yourself to a nice lunch. Wander through an art museum. Visit the museum gift shop and splurge on a thick book of beautiful pictures as a memento of your special day.

Invite! Don't wait until you have the time to prepare a sit-down, gourmet dinner for 10 to ask friends over. Have people who live close-by in for dessert. Serve fruit, nuts, popcorn and juice. Stir up vegies in a wok and cook up brown rice and ask friends to share. Serve baked potatoes with salsa and guacamole toppings and toss a salad. Bring on the company!

"The mind needs to relax by contemplating pictures and other beautiful objects."
                              Maimonides (1135-1204), *Eight Chapters*

Visit art museums. Attend art shows. Stroll through a sculpture garden.

Dress up! Julian is a furniture mover. The owner of a small company, he usually works the van with his crew. That means wearing old clothes and getting dirty and sweaty eight hours a day, five days a week. Two or three week-ends a month, you wouldn't recognize Julian except, of course, for that huge smile. He slides into a three-piece suit, complete with handkerchief in the breast pocket, fastens his initialed cuff links, splashes on cologne and whisks his wife, Clara, off to elegant lunches and dinners, the ballet, plays and dances.

Dress down! Suzy is an attorney. Simeon is a financial analyst. Monday through Friday, the two of them step out of the house, dressed for success, Simeon in his dark, three-piece suit, Suzy in her dress, nylons and heels. The week-end comes, and the tailored look is replaced by shorts or jeans or worn cords, depending upon the weather, t-shirts, sweat shirts, plaid lumberjack shirts and baseball caps. Their action-wear puts them into gear for yard work, playing catch and bike riding with their kids. It's perfect for modeling clay, the family hobby, and for bathing and brushing Crosby, the spunky family mutt and a shaggy dirt collector.

You deserve to have fun today.

Sing,
    dance,
        play,
           laugh,
               draw funny faces.
                    Choose life!

11

Money and Things

"The more we desire the superfluous, the more we meet with difficulties."

        Maimonides (1135-1204), *Guide for the Perplexed*

We asked a group of college students what they wanted out of life. "A mansion with a staff of servants," said one.

"I don't need a mansion," said the second. "A six-bedroom house with a maid and a cook will do fine."

Another student wanted a sports car. "I'm going to get that car before I get married," he said. "No one is going to claim it as community property in a divorce settlement."

One young woman wanted more than anything to be able to open very active charge accounts at every designer shop on Rodeo Drive in Beverly Hills

"Just money, gobs of it; millions is all I require,'" said a garrulous 20-year-old.

When queried why they wanted this wealth, the young men and women responded that these things would make them happy and would make other people think them important.

Are these young people that unusual? How many individuals do you know who measure their dreams and their plans according to the bigger house they're aiming to buy, the new car they hope to have, the boat they're drooling over?

How many shoppers of happiness are constantly prowling the malls, the boutiques, the import shops for that certain something that will deliver bliss?

Maybe that new mulberry sedan will bring happiness. How about the gold-and-emerald necklace? Haven't you seen the television commercial in which a woman purchases a gold bracelet and instantly lifts her depressed spirits?

Money is necessary as a means of exchange to provide shelter, food, clothing and education, together with other essentials and occasional luxuries.

Will more money make you happier?

Are people who sleep in the master bedroom suites of 20-room mansions more content?

Does a $2,500 outfit guarantee a happy wearer?

Do fancy furniture, expensive carpeting and priceless vases insure a cozy, harmonious home?

Do imported linens, fine china and silver always provide warmth at meals?

Why are the newspapers filled with so many stories about rock stars, movie idols, political personalities and wealthy industrialists, people who can immerse themselves in material things, who are drug and alcohol dependent, who suffer depression and even take their own lives?

Don't we all know people like Carl, the 37-year-old plastic surgeon who appears to have everything but the happiness he craves? He's tried luxury hotel getaways, private French lessons, gourmet cooking classes, sleek cars, everything that money can buy in his desperate pursuit of contentment. He tries one thing, and soon it bores him. He sees no purpose to life.

Your value as a human being isn't determined by your bank account or your stock portfolio. In things, people seek tangible verification of themselves; but how can a gold watch or a luxury car or a lavish wine cellar tally the real worth of a person?

"...a person looks on the outward appearance, but the Lord sees into the heart."

adapted from *I Samuel 16:7*

Your happiness can be affected by your attitude toward money and possessions.

"None departs from the world with even half of his or her desires gratified. If he or she has a hundred, they want 200, and if they have 200, they want them doubled again."

adapted from *Ecclesiastes Rabbah*

You have choices about money and things. You can choose how to spend the money you have. You have choices to make about careers; your choices affect your earning potential.

Do you really want the things you maintain you want?

Tamara and Sammy set as their main goal a big house in a fancy suburb. If they could only move to their dream home, they fantasized, they would not only achieve happiness but would show their respective families that they had arrived. So they took out the biggest mortgage the bank would grant and called the movers.

Tamara took one look at their furniture in its new surroundings and felt ill. Although there were many things that she liked, they would just have to go. This new house called for beautiful new things. After all, she conjectured, if people came into the house and saw the old furniture they would realize that she and Sam had, indeed, taken out the biggest mortgage the bank would allow.

She engaged a decorator, who had white carpeting laid on the living room and dining room floors. He brought in sofas and dining chairs in white and various shades of green and gray. He did such a spectacular job that he managed to have an interior design magazine photograph the place.

There were problems. Sammy had to break his habit of putting his feet up on the sofa; total lounging was now out. The three children couldn't be allowed in the living room. The whole family had to eat in the kitchen. And you can guess that red wine, grape juice and raspberry jelly were off the shopping list.

Then Tamara eyed Sammy's treasured 14-year-old Volvo in the driveway. How he loved the car that he had purchased in Sweden, driven around Europe and shipped to the United States. To Tamara, it looked shabby in the driveway, and she was embarrassed when Sammy picked up the kids from Sunday school in it. So, Sam sold his precious Volvo to an eager colleague at work and bought a classy sedan.

The house was a huge one for which to care. A maid was needed twice a week. The white carpeting had to be professionally cleaned every few months. A gardening crew had to be hired. The bills piled up. Sammy, an engineer, had to take on extra consulting jobs to pay the bills. He no longer had the time to poke through used bookstores.

Tamara and Sam didn't own their things. Their things owned them and, in effect, kept them in bondage. Each thing that lured them tightened that bondage.

Do we really need furniture upon which our children can't sit?

Do we need carpeting so thick our guests feel intimidated by it?

How many outfits can we wear at once?

How many necklaces will fit around our necks?

At how many fancy restaurants do we have to dine?

Will we ever find just the right bauble to enchant us for life?

We are not advocating poverty. A life of comfort is one thing. A life in pursuit of solely materialistic goals is quite another.

"Labor ennobles."
Talmud: Nedarim, 49b

You spend so much of your time working to earn money. You deserve to feel good about your job.

You should feel that you are doing something society needs. You should know that your work doesn't exploit others.

You should derive pleasure from your work.

You should be compensated fairly.

You should feel that you are being honest with yourself and with others.

If your job doesn't provide you with these things, consider your options for change.

Take advantage of educational opportunities, training programs that will fortify you with marketable skills. If work or raising a family prevent you from attending classes as a full-time student, go part-time. Check out campus child care facilities or co-operative baby-sitting arrangements.

Don't select a job for its title and status. You will bring the status to the job.

Be proud of yourself!

Our society thrives on the skills of farmers, salespeople, teachers, plumbers, carpenters, lawyers, engineers, bankers, writers, musicians, artists, hair stylists, designers, social workers, restaurateurs, clergy, health professionals, car mechanics, miners, to name a few.

We need each other to build, plant, harvest, sew, package, cook, manufacture, report, educate, publish, market, assemble, design, nurse, entertain, distribute.

There's a Yiddish proverb that says, "Look for your cake and lose your bread."

A job taken just for the material rewards could bring grief.

Bart enjoyed his position as a psychologist with a private counseling group. He relished working with the clients. And he looked forward to the breaks and lunches he would share with his colleagues. Usually, they would brown-bag it in the cushy, comfortable, wood-paneled conference room. Sometimes, they would eat in the atrium. A couple of times a week, they would gather at a quaint neighborhood restaurant, maybe Japanese or Chinese, or at a salad bar.

Bart dressed comfortably for work. He loved his casual denim, corduroy or chinos with a sportcoat. He carried a tie in his pocket.

At a family gathering, Cousin Robert suggested that Bart apply for the position of corporate psychologist which Robert's company was establishing. "It would mean a lot more money," Robert advised him. Bart decided to apply, and he landed the position.

After a few months on the job, Bart sensed a gnawing depression within him. He took an objective look at what had happened.

Each day, he was eating expensive lunches at posh restaurants with the corporate executives who expected him to join them.

He squirmed in the three-piece suits for which he had laid out a small fortune. He missed his comfortable clothes.

While some of the people had serious personal problems which Bart felt he could help solve, many came to seek his counsel on how to jockey for position on the corporate totem pole. They wanted psychological insights to learn how to outmaneuver other employees.

The late hours at the corporate headquarters broke into his early evening jogging. By the time he got home, it was too late, too dark. So, he joined an expensive, indoor tennis club for exercise.

Everyone bucking for position at the corporation worked until 8 p.m. Many came in on weekends. Bart remembered how his father never had time for him. Now, his time with his family was being cut short.

The new position with more money had become a financial as

well as emotional drain.

Bart had the gumption to analyze his situation, decide to make a break and investigate the chance of returning to his former position. He was welcomed back.

"If you can't have what you want, want what you can have."
Solomon ben Judah ibn Gabirol (c.1020-c.1057), *Ethics*

How fortunate is the person who enjoys what he or she has. We have observed people who have substantial incomes but draw less pleasure from their abundance than people who have a fraction of their resources.

Warn your children not to be dazzled by fame and wealth, says the *Apocrypha*.

Geoffrey is a high school history teacher. His wife, Ali, is a counselor at a women's center. They both love their work, crave the involvement with others and feel that they are having a positive effect on people's lives. Their careers are rewarding in every way but financial. However, by choosing wisely they are able to afford a lovely lifestyle.

They and their children, Karen, 10, and Todd, 14, live in a modest three-bedroom tract house. Geoff and Ali learned how to paint and wallpaper. The dining room is a combination dining room and library. Blue book shelves sitting on brackets and standards line two walls, top to bottom. The living room is the living room, den and family room.

The family loves art, and frequently the four of them go to museums and art fairs. Expensive original art is hardly within their reach, yet art adorns their home. Ceramic pots from student sales line two of the dining room shelves. Blown-up travel photographs taken by Geoffrey and Ali hang on the walls together with drawings and collages created by Karen and

Todd. These are augmented by seven watercolors purchased at community art fairs and two Georgia O'Keeffe posters, one depicting the hills near the artist's home in Abiquiu, New Mexico.

Family council meetings have determined money spent on household help could be better spent on week-end getaways. Everyone has chores, and all are involved in meal preparation.

They eat dinner out once a week, preferring to spend money for tickets to plays, concerts and professional basketball games. Usually, the family gathers in the kitchen an hour before dinner to prepare the meal, with tasks for each of the four assigned in advance. They have estimated that their vegetarian diet saves them thousands of dollars a year. Most nights, dinner is eaten in the dining room. Music of the great composers, among them Mendelssohn, Bruckner, Strauss, provides background.

Geoffrey and Ali's jobs don't require extensive and expensive wardrobes. This, and the family's non-indulgence in fancy bedding and household goods, allowed the four of them to travel to Israel last year for Todd's Bar Mitzvah.

They do love to travel. Summer typically calls for piling in the van and touring the United States, often camping en route. The van allows Buckminster, the dog, to accompany them.

They visit the library together at least once a week, selecting one or two books for each member of the family.

They play board games. They crack nuts and roast them.

They spend several evenings a week popping popcorn and playing music.

Both parents could earn extra money by taking on additional

work assignments, but they have chosen not to. Geoff says family is top priority. "The days will pass swiftly, and Karen and Todd will be grown up, before we turn around."

The children, who have been taught that they can earn money for things they want, are self-assured, as they are fortified with a variety of survival skills, everything from sewing buttons to cooking batches of chili. They have learned how to make choices about money.

When the children grow up, Geoff and Ali might consider applying their new-found decorating skills to buying an old house and fixing it up for resale; but that's in the future. Today is what counts in this snuggly household.

Joel and Sharon have been in a position to make very different decisions about money. Successful architects who owned their firm, they didn't have Elliot until Joel was 47 and Sharon was 38. By this time, they had earned substantial disposable income, which allowed them some very creative choices about its use.

They added a wing to the building which housed their firm. Here was the nursery which later became a playroom. When Elliot turned 5, his parents decided to segue from full-time careers to a family-centered lifestyle. They sold their offices and trimmed their client load to several projects a year, which they could carry out from the home offices they built. Their money allowed them to shift their priorities to Elliot and community interests. They offered *pro bono* time to help a housing project happen for the poor.

Choices in how money can be spent is evident when we compare the spending habits of Jory and Lydia. Both women have the same jobs and earn the same salaries. Jory drives a good, used car, carries lunch four days a week, does her own housework, has several good mix-and-match outfits and always looks terrific, has season's tickets to her favorite theatre series, takes a yoga class, has a savings account, owns a condo, is enrolled in several week-end ski trips during the winter and flies off on a major trip once a year.

Lydia opted for a new car, eats all lunches and most dinners out, many in trendy restaurants, is a patsy for a new outfit and has closets bulging with clothes. Her carpeting, furniture, stemware and crystal are pricey. She has a cleaning person for her rented apartment weekly. She can't manage to save for a down payment on a condominium. Her favorite hobby is shopping. She lives from paycheck to paycheck. Her limited traveling consists of visits to a spa which specializes in weight reduction. (The restaurants promptly put the weight back on.) When she lost a job a few years ago, she had to turn to her parents, both retired, to bail her out of financial straits.

How do you treat money? Do you manage money instead of letting it manage you?

Do you choose to eat out less, car pool and do your own home maintenance in order to save the money that will ease the stress of emergencies?

Do you require more money for your lifestyle? If so, do you choose to get the training you need to advance to a different position or change careers?

Do you choose to take on additional work to increase your income?

Can you find good in what you have?

The choice is yours.

12

Nice Folks Finish First

"Ah, those who call evil good
And good evil;
Who present darkness as light
And light as darkness;
Who present bitter as sweet
And sweet as bitter."

Isaiah 5:20

"The work of righteousness shall be peace, and the effect of righteousness, calm and confidence forever."

Isaiah 32:17

An industrial company pours chemical waste into a river that flows by a middle-income housing development. The elementary school the children attend sits close to the river bank. So do a large playground and baseball diamond. At the same time the children read, write, solve mathematical problems, draw, sing, run, swing, slide, catch, bat and chase, they are breathing in the noxious pollutants.

As they romp through what should be the carefree days of innocence, a significant number of them develop cancer. Environmentalists, epidemiologists and medical doctors support the parents' claims that the chemical waste is to blame for the scourge.

To refute the charges, the chemical conglomerate brings out its big public relations guns. The word wizards dash to their computer keyboards and tap out saccharine prose about how much the company loves children and families and the environment. They prep the company CEO for media bites in which he proclaims the corporation's innocence together with his personal sadness for the anguished families.

The preppers are real pros, who anticipate every question a journalist could pose. They coach their players how to dodge probing queries, how to replace self-incriminating answers with slick retorts devoid of substance. The front-liners learn to dart around the interviewers' investigation, utilizing emotional shenanigans as they attempt to manipulate their audiences into perceiving that all they desire is the public good.

Newspapers and investigative television news shows are crammed with stories such as this one. The stuff of dirty deals and swindles, of schemes and chicanery makes good copy. But it doesn't make for happy, peaceful living.

The fast buck, the scam, the "I'll get mine no matter what" attitude, drives some individuals in all walks of life to discount the pain and suffering of other people, animals and the environment whom they stomp on their way to the riches. They feel that so long as they keep polishing their public images, all is well, but it rarely is. For such persons, happiness remains elusive.

"He slays his neighbor who takes away his living."
Apocrypha: Ben Sira 34:22

A business manager manages to pay the mortgage on his glitzy house with money entrusted to him by his clients.

A fast-talking hustler pounces on senior citizens, embezzling their life savings.

A company hires a battery of attorneys to block union-negoti-ated employee pay raises, stripping the workers of their just earnings.

A wheeler-dealer uses questionable money to buy a company, then proceeds to raid its employee pension fund.

"Better a little with righteousness
Than a large income with injustice."

Proverbs 16:8

A doctor persuades a woman to have a hysterectomy, not because she requires one, but because he's stacked up some gambling debts for which payment is due.

A landlord rationalizes that the tenants who live in his slums wouldn't appreciate repairs, so why bother to make them?

A college student boosts her income by selling cocaine. "They'll be buying it from somebody; I might as well stash the cash," she figures.

Money isn't the only thing a person can steal.

A smug college student buys a term paper and turns it in to his English professor.

A narcissistic Lothario charms and leads on lonely women for sex.

Arrogant researchers at an East Coast medical school murder 300 dogs in demonstrating that it takes less electricity applied directly to the head to kill a dog who is stressed by being

109

suspended in a body sling than it does to kill a dog resting peacefully in a cage -- and justify the killings in the name of human health and welfare.

An employer, whose own self-esteem is low, sexually harasses an employee.

A person derives entertainment from gossiping about a neighbor's misfortune.

A tenured teacher swindles her students by never updating her lectures.

On a whim, a couple gets a puppy, comes home and plops the wiggly, loving ball of fur into the arms of their young child. They don't train the pup, ignore her, yell about her canine mistakes, then cast the young dog, who is desperate for human companionship, into the yard and finally oust the confused dog from the family altogether.

"Happy are they who are upright in the way."

Psalms 119:1

Why dwell on all of this unpleasant stuff in a book about happiness? Because a person can't run enough miles, gaze at enough trees, whittle enough wood, observe enough Sabbaths or do any of the things we recommend for a happy life in an effort to erase the gnawing inner sense that something is missing, if that person is unethical in his or her dealings with others.

Such a person might appear luminous and fulfilled on the outside, draped in designer costumes, even the recipient of public accolades, but something will be missing inside, the inner peace necessary for contentment.

"Observe what is right and do what is just," proclaimed the prophet Isaiah (*56:1*).

A better world begins with each one of us.

We can choose to accept that design or ignore it. "What is hateful to you do not do to anyone. That is the whole Torah. The rest is commentary," said Hillel 2,000 years ago.

13

"Tikkun" Is Never Boring

"Thus says the Lord: Do justice and right; rescue from the defrauder him who is wronged; do not exploit or harm the stranger, the orphan or the widow, and do not shed the blood of the innocent in this place."

Jeremiah 22.3

Apathy, ennui and malaise can be your greatest impediments in the search for personal happiness.

How many times have we heard: "I have everything: a successful career . . . a beautiful family . . . a more-than-comfortable house and a vacation condo. . . .an attention-getting car. I take fabulous vacations . . . wear designer clothes . . .have sound equipment that transforms my home into Avery Fischer Hall . . . am able to afford orchestra seats to all the stellar shows."

But -- and it is a BIG BUT: "The excitement of a new car doesn't last long . . . I'm bored with haute cuisine. . . . The world's top vacation spots are all beginning to look alike. I'm blase; bored, bored, bored!"

An old Yiddish folk saying puts it this way: *Es fehlt a bissel feffer; es fehlt a bissel zaltz.* Your life lacks a bit of pepper; it lacks a bit of salt! Your life may be boring and bland, nothing more than a stifled yawn.

What's missing to spice things up? Rabbi Hillel, who lived in the Land of Israel at the beginning of the first century, taught:
"If I am not for myself, who is for me?
If I care only for myself, what am I?
If not now, when?"

Pirke Avot, 1:14

The price that is exacted from us for not wanting to relate to the problems and the plight of others in our society and in the world is a heavy one. We become isolated from people and values; and no amount of creature comforts can mask the loneliness and emptiness of our lives.

In the spring of 1989, People's Republic of China troops destroyed the "Goddess of Democracy" statue as part of their bloody suppression of a mass protest by students in Beijing's Tian An Men Square. When sympathetic artists erected a replica of the statue in Los Angeles' Chinatown, it was destroyed by vandals.

Many Angelenos greeted with concern and indignation the news that the symbol of peace and democracy had been sabotaged. Newspaper accounts of the day, however, reported that others expressed indifference.

"I just don't care," one citizen was quoted as saying. "I just want to lead a normal life."

The attribution was painfully reminiscent of the tragic parallel of Katherine Genovese, who was stabbed repeatedly on a street near her home in the New York borough of Queens after nightfall on a summer's evening.

Kitty's repeated cries for help were ignored by the residents of the apartment buildings surrounding the area where the assault was taking place. They simply shut their windows, even though it was a warm evening, drew their blinds and chose to watch TV to drown out Kitty's cries, until there remained only silence and Kitty's corpse.

Kitty Genovese's body has long been moldering in her grave; but her fate remains a powerful commentary on those individuals who choose not to become "involved."

One of the songs to emerge from the concentration camps of the Holocaust is called "Es Brentt!" ("It's Burning!") The Yiddish lyrics tell of a *shtetl*, a small Jewish village somewhere in Eastern Europe, that is being put to the torch by the Nazis. While everyone stands around with folded hands, doing nothing but gaping, the village is aflame. The song points out dramatically that our entire world is afire -- and nothing is being done to contain the conflagration..

If you choose not to become "involved," not to commit yourself, not to give of yourself to something greater than your private goals and ambitions, the result, inevitably, has to be ennui, burnout and malaise, detours in your search for happiness.

On Yom Kippur, the Day of Atonement, the most solemn occasion in the Jewish religious calendar, the liturgy contains the following passage:

"... this is the fast I desire:
To unlock the fetters of wickedness,
And untie the cords of the yoke.
To let the oppressed go free;
To break off every yoke.
It is to share your bread with the hungry,
And to take the wretched poor into your home..."

Isaiah 58:6

Near the conclusion of every Jewish worship service -- daily,

115

"Tikkun" Is Never Boring

Sabbath, Festival and High Holy Days -- there is a prayer called the *Ah-LAY-noo*, in which we are called upon to "repair and heal the world under the kingdom of God."

This concept, which is known in Hebrew as *Tikkun Olam*, is the basis of the Jewish belief in involvement not only as a moral obligation but as a pathway to personal happiness and a sense of self-fulfillment.

If you are truly down in the dumps, the quickest remedy we can prescribe is to perform an immediate good deed, a *mitzvah* :
• Call a sick friend or neighbor and find out how he or she is.
• Offer to shop for someone who can't get out.
• Phone an elderly relative or neighbor just to say "Hello" and let them know that you are thinking about them. Send them birthday cards.
• Gather a collection of canned goods and take them to a certified depository for the poor.
• Find out if there are youngsters who need rides to your synagogue youth group meetings.
• Whip up a colorful salad. Warm up a loaf of bread. Take them to the home of someone who is caring for a sick relative. Help the care-giver.
• Invite a recently-widowed friend to dinner.
• Listen to someone who is hurting.
• Find out if the children at the local hospital can use your read magazines for cut and paste projects Take a bundle over.
• Walk a dog whose human companion is ill.
• Cram your piles of newspapers into bags and cart them to a recycling center.
• If you decide to adopt an animal companion, go to an animal shelter or rescue group. Save a life.
• Invite someone who lives alone to a holiday dinner.
• Welcome that new person who's been attending services. Introduce him or her to others.

"...what the Lord requires of you:
Only to do justice
And to love goodness,
And to walk humbly with your God..."

Micah, 6:8

A precondition to personal happiness is your involvement in the struggle for justice in a world where greed enables people to rationalize their mistreatment of others, the greed that bestows power on some and makes victims of others.

It may seem contradictory to link the words "happiness" and "struggle," as we have just done. The apparent contradiction is easily resolved: you can't experience true happiness unless it is coupled with an inner glow that comes from knowing that you have not turned away from the realities of the world but have taken your place in the arena where the battle goes on for the dignity and integrity of all of God's creatures, human and animal.

Just ask yourself: How can I be happy when I blot out the reality that:
people die of hunger?
children are abused?
women are beaten and raped?
animals are tortured?
people are executed because of their political beliefs?
illiteracy sits astride the world like a black shadow?
the rain forests, our entire planet Earth, are being savaged?

By getting involved, you create the possibility of change, you provide hope, and that is life-affirming. And by getting involved you join others who share your sensitivities and form a strong support group.

"The merciful person does good to his or her own soul."

adapted from *Proverbs 11:17*

"Tikkun" Is Never Boring

In addition to individual acts of compassion, you may want to attain the happiness that results from personal fulfillment by identifying with commanding issues that are on the agenda of *Tikkun Olam*, healing of society through social justice.

Here is a partial list of issues that cry out for your involvement:
• Racism
• Arms control
• Nuclear power
• Low-income housing and homelessness
• Black-Jewish relations
• Civil rights
• Women's rights
• Animal rights
• Migrant farm workers
• Israel, the West Bank and Gaza Strip
• World hunger and famine
• Reproductive rights
• Better child care
• Drug and alcohol abuse and traffic
• Education and functional illiteracy
• Saving the environment
• Improving the quality of life for the disabled
• Protection of the First Amendment

A big order? Too much to swallow? Remember:
"You are not called upon to complete the task, but neither are you free to evade it."
Ethics of the Fathers, 3:21

Look at some of the things you can do to help:

• Volunteer to staff a rape hotline.
• Volunteer to staff a child abuse hotline.
• Volunteer to staff a crisis hotline.
• Sign up to defeat illiteracy. Call your local library for details,

and watch a human being gain dignity before your eyes.
• Join a hunger project.
• Read to the blind.
• Help train kids for Special Olympics.
• Volunteer at a home for the aged. Just chatting with some of the residents will brighten their days.
• Help out at an animal shelter.
• Find out if the local shelter for battered women needs your help.
• Find out if the elementary school in your area has a foster grandparent program.
• Organize a food and clothing drive in your neighborhood for the community project for the homeless.
• Volunteer at a hospital.
• Become a Big Brother.
• Become a Big Sister.
• Write letters supporting your causes to legislators.
• Write letters of protest to companies that exploit people, the environment and animals.
• Organize letter-writing campaigns.
• Attend rallies.
• Mount petition drives.

Choose life for others, life free of pain, suffering and humiliation. In so doing, you will be choosing life for yourself as well.

We have never seen it fail. Those we know who get involved in *Tikkun Olam* through commitment to overriding social issues are happier than others who are involved solely with themselves.

Two of the happiest men with whom we ever had the privilege of spending time were Poul Borchsenius and Jens Lillelund. One was a Lutheran pastor in Denmark who gained the name of "the fighting priest" during World War II. The other, Lillelund, was one of the leaders of the Danish resistance to the

"Tikkun" Is Never Boring

Nazis who occupied his homeland.

Together, they were among the heroes who rescued almost the entire Jewish population of Denmark from under the very noses of the Gestapo just before Rosh Hashanah of 1943 and spirited them across the Sund to neutral Sweden.

An important part of their adult lives had been spent in fighting the Nazi invader and risking their lives in the process. But they were happy, self-fulfilled men.

The happiest, most fulfilled people we have met are those who have devoted time and energy to helping others. Some have mobilized movements; others have volunteered a few hours a week to doing for others.

Two hours a week of your time could make the difference in the life of a person who is unable to read.

One hour of holding your hand and listening to your voice could comfort a lonely person facing surgery.

A few hours spent calling neighbors and collecting children's clothes could result in sending a homeless child off to school with some dignity.

The two hours a week you spend at an animal shelter could help reunite lost animals with their distraught families.

The letter you write your legislator might be the final salvo needed for her to switch her vote on a bill that would protect a forest preserve.

For all of us who wish to link our search for happiness with concern for helping others, the mandate is unmistakeable, and the agenda is obvious. Wherever and whenever we raise our voices and place our bodies in behalf of the abused and tormented of God's living beings, there we belong.

For Jews, there is a special dimension to the challenge of *Tikkun Olam*, to "heal the world." A grim by-product of the Holocaust was the silence of peoples, their governments and their churches, while millions of Jews and others were consumed. Now, Jews dare not turn away or stifle their outrage while injustice persists.

Tikkun Olam is never boring!

14

Claim Your Identity

"Blessed are those who keep the foundations of their fore-bears."

adapted from *Apocrypha: II Enoch 52.9*

In July of 1971, on the last day of our honeymoon, we were driving west across the island of Hawaii to the airport at Hilo when we came across a little-known, small museum, privately maintained.

Housed in an old mansion, the museum was a treasure trove of Hawaiian memorabilia, historic documents, artifacts and sea shells of all sizes, shapes and colors.

We were the only visitors that afternoon, so the proprietor, who appeared to be a full-blooded native islander, was eager to show us around and answer our questions.

When he discovered that Sid was a rabbi, he told us that his grandfather, a Jewish peddler, had come to the islands from his native Syria on a Clipper ship in the 1880s. Grandfather had met and married a native Hawaiian. Our host was a descendant of that union.

He took a key out of his pocket and opened a glass display cabinet. Reaching in, he removed one of the precious shells and handed it to us. "Please accept this gift," he said. "My grandfather would have wanted me to give a gift to a rabbi."

We are, each one of us, connected to the history of humankind and to the history of of our forebears. We are not isolated entities floating through a short span of time. We are linked to the generations. Each of us has a heritage tied to our family, our religion, our ethnicity. It is good to know who you are, where you came from, to know that you belong to something.

In recent years, increasing numbers of people, many in their 20s, 30s and 40s, have been flocking to the antique shops, auctions, second-hand stores, flea markets and estate sales. In their search for clocks and chairs, pendants and portraits, saucers, cups, plates and toys, they are hoping to discover not only the designs and workmanship of the past but also to fulfill their own yearnings for connections to bygone days.

Customs and traditions also connect us to other generations. We can adopt or adapt those handed down to us by our parents, grandparents and great-grandparents and thereby link us to them, at the same time providing us with a sense of identity, an awareness of roots.

We can augment those customs handed down to us with some we establish in our own homes. Whether your family consists of just you or you and others, you can establish customs.

When we recite the blessings for the Sabbath, the New Year, the Festivals and other holidays, we are joined to our people throughout the centuries who recited them, to those proud faces in the worn photos in your picture album and to all who came before them. When we listen to the shrill sounds of the *shofar* on Rosh Hashanah, we are connected again. Next time you light the Sabbath tapers or sing the Hanukkah blessings, try to picture your loved ones who are no longer here.

124

Every time we sit down in our home at the Passover *seder*, Sid recalls his parents, aunts and uncles, of blessed memory, who occupied places around the Passover banquet tables of his childhood and youth. He recounts nostalgically and with a mixture of wistfulness and humor the exchanges and other incidents around the *seder* table.

Our *seders* are different from the ones they experienced. The food is good but simple and underplayed. Baked potatoes and gobs of fresh vegetables and fruits make up the repast. Since we are vegetarians, a beet and sprouts replace the shank bone and egg on the *seder* plate. But the matzah is there, and the *haroset* and the bitter herbs and the singing and the love. And their spirits are there, their impact felt on Sid and each one of us.

We have heard people say that customs and traditions are restrictive. To the contrary, they can be exhilarating, something upon which you can depend. They can warm you and sustain you.

It is fascinating to learn about the peoples of the world, to witness their lifestyles, to hear their music, to watch their dances, to taste their food. It is astonishing to hear about their struggles and their triumphs.

It is all the more incredible to learn of our own people.

A strip of Fairfax avenue between Beverly boulevard and Melrose avenue in Los Angeles has long been home for immigrant Jews from Eastern Europe. Most of them are elderly. Canes and walkers add to the sidewalk gridlock along the rows of delicatessens, bakeries, produce markets, bookstores, Israeli cafes, beauty parlors, discount outlets and newsstands.

Men with bristle on their chins stand on the street corners, their bodies gesticulating in every possible way as they debate world events. Women, whose oversize handbags and shopping bags almost overshadow their owners' shrinking frames, wobble into stores they have patronized for decades.

We brought a young friend, who is not Jewish, to the Beverly-Fairfax neighborhood. He had never seen a concentration number emblazoned on someone's arm before. He saw it here. On Sundays, younger Jews from the Westside and San Fernando Valley drive here, park on the side streets and follow the aromas of warm rye bread and bagels and spicy kosher dills. They come not only to eat but to listen. It won't be long before we will no longer hear the Yiddish accents.

We join them all. In our Sunday outfits of safari-style pants with the six pockets, the colorful epaulet shirts and the multi-pocketed vests, we walk among them. We look different. We sound different. We are all the same. We are they, and they are us. The thought is a comforting one.

In the summer of 1973, during a visit to Denmark, Norway and Finland, we found ourselves in Tampere, 187 kilometers northwest of Helsinki by rail. Placed on a slender isthmus crossed by the Tammerkaski rapids, which journey from the Nasijarvi to Lake Pyhajarvi, it claims rightfully to be "a modern town with wide esplanades, parks and notable examples of 20th century Finnish architecture and sculpture."

But a Jewish community? Acting upon a clue in a tour guidebook, we found ourselves in the Tampereen Juutalaineh Seurakunta, an impressive designation for the Jewish community center, housed in an apartment.

Never a huge Jewish community, the Jewish congregation of Tampere had now shrunk to some 25 persons in 12 families. When we sought out the president of the Jewish community, we learned that he was entertaining a couple who had left the town some years before to settle in Israel. We were invited to participate in the reunion at a local restaurant. Upon our joining them, we found the host and his guests from Israel well-warmed by rounds of vodka toasts -- which were renewed with our late arrival.

Until the restaurateur politely and patiently stood by our table in his now-deserted establishment in the early hours of the morning, we engaged in animated exchanges. It was an unlikely gathering of people: a writing team (one member of which was a rabbi) from the United States; the elderly presiding officer of this Finnish *kehillah*; his son, a wireless operator on a transoceanic vessel, at home on vacation, and the Tampere expatriates, now living in Israel.

Among us, we resorted to four languages to communicate with each other: Yiddish, Hebrew, English and Finnish. We grew adept at this mishmash of tongues, even telling jokes and getting the punch lines across.

Our conversation was by no means all frivolous. We talked a great deal about Israel, of course, its problems and the divisions between the ultra-religious and secular segments of its polyglot Jewish population; the prospects, or lack of them, for peace with its Arab neighbors; the probabilities of survival for Diaspora Jewry, a poignant discussion considering the demographics of the Tampere Jewish community.

Throughout, there was a community of interest among us, despite the language barriers and the differences in our respective backgrounds. We were all family members, part of the "in-group," and we felt completely at home with these new-found "relatives."

This is what is meant by ethnicity, identity and continuity.

Find out who you are. Find out what went into the making of the very special person, you. Collect all the information you can. Interview older relatives. Encourage them to share their memories. Ask them to describe the photographs in the albums. If you can get the family elders to be specific, you might want to pencil in notes on the reverse sides of the pictures, identifying persons, dates, places and occasions.

Make use of state-of-the-art electronic aids to record for posterity. Camcorder interviews are excellent for oral/visual family histories. If the interviewee is self-conscious, an audio tape recorder can be a practical compromise.

The process of interviewing the surviving "old-timers" need not be a somber, formal one. Many of their anecdotal reminiscences will prove hilarious. Example: try to determine if first or surnames emerged intact from the immigration process at Ellis Island. Or did "Yankele" end up as "John Kelly"? Sid's father was brought to the United States as an infant by his non-English speaking parents. When immigration officials asked for the baby's name, they were told that it was "Menachem Mendel," whereupon the little one was promptly dubbed "Emanuel," a name which he carried all his life.

Give your children a history of family, so that they will have a sense of self.

15

The Pause That Makes for Happiness

"This is the meaning of the Jewish Sabbath, to give to (a person) peaceful hours, hours completely diverted from everyday life, seclusion from the world in the midst of the world."

Rabbi Leo Baeck (1873-1956),
The Essence of Judaism

"More than Israel has kept the Sabbath, the Sabbath has kept Israel."

Ahad Ha'am (Hebrew essayist, 1856-1927),
Al Parashat Derachim

All week long, we work, cope with the world, barter and exchange goods and services. We are caught up in the whirlwind of the marketplace. We are saturated with all that is mercantile.

When we ring up the list of obligations we have to fulfill in order to sustain our physical lives, it's no wonder so many of us feel overwhelmed. We have our jobs. We must shop for groceries and incidentals. We need to pick up screws at the hardware store. And, surely, someone in the household has run out of underwear or socks. The car needs gas and oil changes and repairs and emission checks. We have a yen for new wallpaper and paint to remodel the bathroom. Light bulbs are to be changed, the garbage taken out, the plumber called.

What a terrific idea the Sabbath is, the opportunity to rejuvenate the spirit, to recharge our batteries. You might say that if the Sabbath day did not exist someone would have to invent it.

Isn't it great to pull back on the seventh day, to bask in being, not doing? There are many ways you can plug this refresher into your life.

This day of "delight," as Isaiah called it (58.13), was a revolutionary idea in Biblical times. To those of you caught up in the fast lane of today's high-tech, competitive society, it might be just the therapy for the twin ills of burnout and malaise.

Shabbat, the Jewish Sabbath, begins at sundown Friday and lasts until the first stars appear on Saturday. Some Jews attend synagogue services on Friday nights and Saturday mornings. The Sabbath Eve dinner is a time for family and friends to get together and join in the singing of Sabbath songs and revel in the warmth and joy of their relationships.

Orthodox Jews refrain from conducting business or doing anything that can be construed as work on the Sabbath. On this day, they don't even carry money on their person. Shopping for anything is out. They travel only by walking, usually to synagogue and then to the homes of neighbors, friends or relatives where they might gather for lunch, study and conversation. The telephone goes unanswered. The turning on of electricity is forbidden. That means a break from television, computers and kitchen appliances. Cooked foods such as the traditional *cholent*, a tasty stew easily made with potatoes, beans and vegetables, are prepared in advance. It is a beautiful time for spiritual renewal and family bonding.

Conservative Jews are expected to follow the same regimen, although driving to synagogue services is permitted. Persons who are affiliated with the Reform and Reconstructionist denominations in Judaism take a less restrictive view of Sabbath observance. For instance, they might celebrate the Sabbath afternoon by listening to a Metropolitan Opera radio broadcast or by attending a museum exhibition or a matinee performance at the theatre.

The Sabbath can be a weekly spiritual vacation during which there is no preoccupation with things and accomplishments, only with existence.

Think about it. If you don't go shopping one day, that's the day on which you won't experience the minor irritations that so often accompany trips to the mall, the supermarket and decorators' row.

Many perceive the Sabbath as a 24-hour period of "cannots"; it is actually a period of "cans."

At sunset, you can begin the Sabbath with the lighting of candles. The kindling of those tapers and the blessings that accompany it connect us with all of our relatives who are no longer with us, with those of whom we have cherished memories and with those who came before them. We are bonded at that moment with Jews in every place and in every time. We skirt the centuries and become part of the adventure that is Jewish history.

You can make a blessing (*Kiddush*) over wine or fruit juice and express gratitude for the bounty that is spread on your table.

You can sing special Sabbath songs (*z'mirot*).

You can enjoy a peaceful meal by yourself. Or, you can invite others to join you. Jack, a bachelor, traditionally invites

131

friends over on Friday evening. He cooks up a stew on Thursday night, then fixes the salad and washes the fresh fruit on Friday when he comes home from work. Sabbath meals need not be elaborate. Simple is easier and healthier.

You can share your thoughts about the week that has passed and indulge in speculation about the week ahead.

You can attend Friday evening services at synagogue. There is no admission fee.

You can spend the evening in conversation, discussing ideas.

You can read.

You can enjoy music.

Saturday morning, you can attend synagogue services. Again, no charge.

You can spend the day in private study or prayer.

You can have friends over for lunch.

You can visit an art museum or the ballet or attend a matinee performance of a play.

As the first stars appear on Saturday evening, the Sabbath is ushered out with a beautiful ceremony, appropriately called *Havdalah* (separation). Utilizing a special, multi-colored, braided candle, wine and spice box, the *Havdalah* ceremony marks the division between the Sabbath and the rest of the week, the sacred and the secular.

When the candle flame is doused in a saucer containing some of the wine, and *Shah-voo-ah Tove* ("a Good Week") is sung, the Sabbath is officially at an end.

The town of Barstow, in the High Desert of California, has only 12 Jewish families; but it has managed for many years to have a functioning synagogue, housed in its own tiny but homey structure. One of Sid's most pleasant professional experiences was the year he served Congregation Beth Israel as its non-resident rabbi. On Saturday evenings, the entire Jewish community gathers in a circle outside the synagogue and joins hands for a Havdalah ceremony under the stars. What a simple yet majestic setting in which to usher out the Sabbath and, at the same time, bind the Jewish community into an extended family!

The basic idea is to remove yourself from the commercial world as much as possible.

Some cynics say that if you don't observe the Sabbath the way the Orthodox do, why bother at all? This is the "all or nothing at all" syndrome. It is a cop-out; take it, and you end up with zilch in terms of your personal happiness and growth.

"The Sabbath is the day of peace between people and nature. . . By not working -- by not participating in the process of natural and social change -- (a person) is free from the chains of nature and from the chains of time, although only for one day a week."

Erich Fromm (1900-1980),
The Forgotten Language

Judaism sees in the Sabbath an opportunity for the individual, stripped of the constraints of being bound to the marketplace or the kitchen, to get in touch with himself or herself. It is not accidental that Saturday afternoon, after the return from synagogue services and Sabbath lunch, is viewed in Judaism as a propitious time for making love to one's husband or wife!

It isn't surprising then, is it, that the utter relaxation and spiritual indulgence of *Shabbat* is seen as a hint of how life might be in the Messianic era, the time when, as Jewish tradition puts it so succinctly, *"yome sheh-koo-low Shabbat,"* the days of our lives will be all Sabbath.

16

The Power That Makes for Happiness

A book whose theme is the search for and attainment of happiness must, inevitably, lay itself open to the charge of hedonism, the belief that happiness or pleasure is the highest good. We usually associate hedonism with the pursuit of pleasure for pleasure's own sake, with narcissism and with selfishness.

The extra something that distinguishes this book from being a trivial pursuit of happiness is an awareness of a Power or Process Beyond Ourselves, which we designate as God.

We skirt the danger of being pedantic by injecting God and prayer into our up-to-now rational discussion of attaining happiness. At the same time, we are aware that the ultimate source of personal happiness derives from a Power Greater than Ourselves.

The twin dragons of alienation and loneliness stand in the way of your attaining true happiness. They can scuttle the positive interaction between individuals, married persons, parents and children, between siblings, neighbors, business and professional associates.

Henry David Thoreau (1817-62) was writing about most of us when he observed that we "live lives of quiet desperation."

The Power That Makes For Happiness

How can we possibly discover the happiness that comes from self-fulfillment if we must keep searching for some meaning to our existence, if we must keep asking ourselves, "What's it all about?"

If we seek their origins, we have to do some spiritual root-canal digging and discover that alienation and loneliness are the twin by-products of a lack of rootedness in a meaningful and self-fulfilling God concept.

"God is in the faith by which we overcome the fear of loneliness, of helplessness, of failure and of death."
Rabbi Mordecai M. Kaplan (1881-1983),
Jewish Reconstructionist High Holy Day Prayer Book

Frankly, we debated whether to include this chapter in a book on happiness for fear of appearing to come on to you as "preachy," especially when one co-author is a rabbi.

We did not have to struggle long before arriving at our decision. This book is designed to be consistently honest and aboveboard in discussing all phases of the quest for personal happiness, derived from and inspired by Jewish sources. Why, then, do many people you know -- yourself included, perhaps -- try to avoid a belief in or commitment to a Higher Being?

The answer is not difficult to ferret out. Many if not most of us have had our ideas about God frozen at a 5-year-old level. As kids, we may have been fed a pablum of very childish ideas about God by our parents and other relatives.

Unlike other areas of juvenile misinformation, which are cleared up as we grow older, many of our ideas about God have been ossified in their childish state and, consequently, are rejected by our adult minds.

The self-professed atheist, who says he or she denies the idea of God, really rejects the image of the Old Man with the Long, White Beard sitting in Heaven and gazing down blandly -- or malevolently, as the case may be -- on us earthlings.

Judaism is not a religion of dogmas. You are left free to accept any God concept that makes the most sense and is most conducive to your sincerely believing -- provided you remain firm in professing that God is One. At the same time, your God Idea should be the product of your adult mind and not a vestige of the fantasy world of your childhood.

The manner in which people may conceive of God can run a very wide spectrum.

At one polarity is the belief in a supernatural, personal God, a being who is directly concerned with your individual welfare and who intervenes at will in the processes of nature to achieve His desires. This is the God-concept of traditional Judaism that enabled the folk-Jew to address the Deity with the Yiddish word, *tah-teh-noo*, "Daddy."

At the other end of the spectrum is the belief in an impersonal God, the Power that Makes for Good in us. God (He, She or It) acts in and through history, in and through nature and in and through the hearts and psyches of human beings.

Some will elect the approach of mysticism to find God. Others are more comfortable with a highly rational God-concept.

Our spiritual needs are highly individual, terribly intimate. Some of us seek a supernatural deity; others may reflect a very cerebral view of God. In spite of their individual preferences, Jews are comfortable praying to Adonai, the One God, the Source of Good in the world.

Through prayer and meditation, we are reminded to choose good, to choose life, against all the forces -- that is, the lifestyles

-- of darkness.

In all candor, we must admit that there are many people who consider themselves Jews ethnically and culturally, although they are complete non-believers religiously. Some are avowed atheists, who hold that God does not exist. More likely, they may be agnostics, skeptical but ready to admit that they don't know beyond a doubt that there is no God.

A number of leading personalities in modern Jewish history can be considered to have been agnostics, among them the founder and first prime minister of the State of Israel, David Ben Gurion, and one of his successors in that office, Golda Meir, as well as the late United States Supreme Court Justice Louis D. Brandeis.

For our part, we feel the Power or Process of Good within each of us. The more each one of us chooses good, the closer we will be to a Messianic Era.

Admittedly, it is more difficult to pray to the impersonal God than to the Father Deity; but, in our pursuit of happiness and stability, we have to learn to try prayer.

We pray for the power to choose good and to choose life:

"I have put before you life and death, blessing and curse. Choose life. . ."   *Deuteronomy 30:19*

Spending some time each day in visualizing good in the world and asking for strength and courage and energy can be a soothing experience.

"Where can I find You?" asks the Jew in an old, Hassidic song, as he searches for happiness.

"And where can I not find you!" he cries out triumphantly. "Eastward--You! Westward--You! Northward--You! Southward--You!"

Rabbi Kaplan, in the High Holy Day prayerbook of the Reconstructionist movement in Judaism, which he founded, summarized the search for individual salvation and meaning to our existence when he wrote:

"God is the mystery of life, enkindling inert matter with inner drive and purpose."

The guideposts on the road to happiness are clearly marked:

Choose life! Choose good! Choose God!

Afterword

Our message to you has been a simple one: Choose Life!

Get out of you all the best that is in you.

Choose life over things.

Select the true riches of the world from those that have been offered as substitutes for happiness.

Know that you can make a difference in your own life and in the lives of others.

Live each day to the fullest.

Feel vigorous.

Know the peace of the Sabbath, the joy of performing *mitzvot*.

Appreciate your value, your uniqueness.

Love learning, bask in the arts, commune with nature, create, establish goals.

Know the love of others.

Afterword

Know the joy of sharing moments with animals.

Make your mistakes the building blocks of your growth, your achievements the mortar.

Know that your attitudes and the choices you make will set the pattern for your life.

Be outraged at evil and crush it wherever and whenever you can; but recognize good, and delight in it.

Be at one with all that is good; be at one with God.

The people we know who live this way not only derive more from every good experience, but they are better able to cope with disappointment, frustration and even tragedy. Drawing strength from the richness of their lives and their ability to contemplate their options, they triumph over their losses, feeling their pain but able to move forward.

Hold the moment dear. Live hard. Live jubilantly.

Your life is your fortune. Spend it wisely.

Soar with the good that is in you.

Be blessed.

Be cherished.

Be healthy.

Be happy.

Choose Life!